WHY ALFRED BURNED THE CAKES

1. Count Gleichen's statue of Alfred at his birthplace, Wantage (1877), said to be based on the features of Colonel Robert Loyd-Lindsay, the local MP who commissioned it.

PROFILES IN HISTORY

....

WHY ALFRED BURNED THE CAKES

A KING AND HIS ELEVEN-HUNDRED-YEAR AFTERLIFE

DAVID HORSPOOL

P

PROFILE BOOKS

First published in Great Britain in 2006 by
Profile Books Ltd
3A Exmouth House
Pine Street
Exmouth Market
London EC1R 0JH
www.profilebooks.com

1 3 5 7 9 10 8 6 4 2

Typeset in Palatino by MacGuru Ltd
info@macguru.org.uk
Printed and bound in Great Britain by
Clays, Bungay, Suffolk

A CIP catalogue record for this book is available from
the British Library.

ISBN-10: 1 86197 786 7
ISBN-13: 978 1 86197 786 1

For Jules

CONTENTS

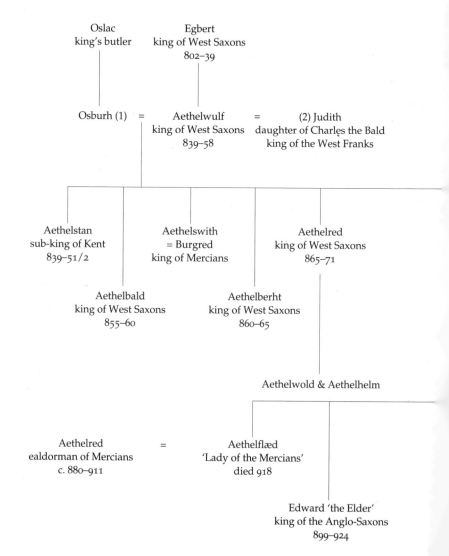

Oslac
king's butler

Egbert
king of West Saxons
802–39

Osburh (1) = Aethelwulf = (2) Judith
king of West Saxons daughter of Charles the Bald
839–58 king of the West Franks

Aethelstan
sub-king of Kent
839–51/2

Aethelswith
= Burgred
king of Mercians

Aethelred
king of West Saxons
865–71

Aethelbald
king of West Saxons
855–60

Aethelberht
king of West Saxons
860–65

Aethelwold & Aethelhelm

Aethelred
ealdorman of Mercians
c. 880–911

= Aethelflæd
'Lady of the Mercians'
died 918

Edward 'the Elder'
king of the Anglo-Saxons
899–924

Alfred's family and genealogy

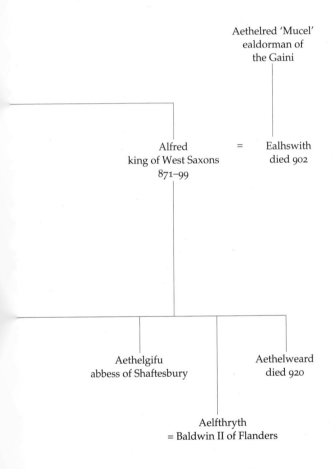

Aethelred 'Mucel'
ealdorman of
the Gaini

Alfred   =   Ealhswith
king of West Saxons   died 902
871–99

Aethelgifu   Aethelweard
abbess of Shaftesbury   died 920

Aelfthryth
= Baldwin II of Flanders

'Historians, you think,' said Miss Tilney, 'are not happy in their flights of fancy. They display imagination without raising interest. I am fond of history – and am very well contented to take the false with the true. In the principal facts they have sources of intelligence in former histories and records, which may be as much depended on, I conclude, as anything that does not actually pass under one's own observation; and as for the little embellishments you speak of, they are embellishments, and I like them as such.'

Jane Austen, *Northanger Abbey* (1818)

INTRODUCTION

IDYLLS OF A KING

This book addresses a moment in history that probably never happened. But the story of Alfred the Great burning the cakes was recounted in dozens of different forms for over a thousand years. Alfred, king of Wessex – who had been fighting the Vikings all his short life, who had watched his father and brothers worn out by the struggle, seen his kinsmen die, his royal counterparts in the other Anglo-Saxon kingdoms of Mercia, East Anglia and Northumbria driven out or martyred and horribly butchered – was on the run. On or about Twelfth Night 878 the Viking army had pounced in a lightning attack on the town of Chippenham, where Alfred and his court were wintering. The West Saxons were taken completely by surprise; there was supposed to be a truce with the enemy, and anyway winter campaigning was unknown. Perhaps the members of Alfred's household were in their cups or suffering the effects of the feasting so memorably described in Anglo-Saxon poetry. Barely managing to escape with his family and a tiny retinue, Alfred holed up in what the annals of the Anglo-Saxon Chronicle, in a rare rhetorical grace-note, memorably call the 'fen-fastnesses' of the Somerset marshes.

The last independent English king appeared down and

out: 878, rather than 1066, might have been remembered as the death year of Anglo-Saxon England. But from a small marsh island called Athelney, Alfred would rebuild his fighting forces and retake his kingdom, after defeating his enemy at the Battle of Edington, in a victory that at last allowed him to impose enduring restrictions on the Vikings. Before this reversal of fortune, however, he had to suffer the ultimate humiliation. Taking refuge in a cowherd's hovel, alone, with no indication of his identity, Alfred was asked to watch the cakes baking in the ashes of the wife's fire. In his *A Child's History of England* (1851–3) Charles Dickens goes on with a typical version of the story:

> being at work on his bow and arrows, with which he hoped to punish the false Danes when a brighter time should come, and thinking deeply of his poor unhappy subjects whom the Danes chased through the land, his noble mind forgot the cakes, and they were burnt. 'What!' said the cowherd's wife, … 'you will be ready enough to eat them by-and-by, and yet you cannot watch them, idle dog?'

There is no contemporary evidence for the cowherd, the hovel, the wife or the cakes. Though there may have been an early oral tradition along these lines, in all likelihood Alfred (849–99) never took solitary shelter in a peasant's cottage, never 'burned the cakes', and the story was probably invented to make an obscure saint associated with Alfred's family look good. The first time it appears written down is in a Life of St Neot, which dates from around a hundred years after Alfred's death. So it may seem obtuse to take a story as thoroughly discredited as that of Alfred and the cakes as the jumping-off point for an examination of a crucial slice of English history.

Modern historians distrust stories. And not only historians: scepticism is generally now taken as a sign of mature good sense. We all tend towards what Simon Schama has called the 'automatic modern assumption of apocrypha' when confronted with a neat historical anecdote. Though the historical profession (and the reading public) appear in recent years to have breathed a collective sigh of relief that narrative has come back into fashion, mere stories – the vignette that sums up a historical character, the moment when a voice from the crowd or a statesman's telling remark gives instant context to the wider picture – are usually debunked, junked as 'later accretions', stamped 'no contemporary evidence' or 'too good to be true'. Of course, that is in one sense very proper. Even those stories with better contemporary corroboration than Alfred and the cakes need to be weighed against other evidence, put into context, scrutinised for who first told them, who popularised them and why. And whatever the supporting evidence (or lack of it), history consisting only of Nero fiddling while Rome burns, of Robert the Bruce and the spider, of admirals playing bowls or holding telescopes to their blind eye would be woefully incomplete. Then again, history that focuses purely on economic data, or diplomatic correspondence, or intelligence signals, will never be complete either.

The story of the cakes is set, chronologically, between two rather better attested events: the Vikings' driving out of Alfred and his followers from Chippenham about Twelfth Night 878 and the mustering of a force to meet them in battle, at Edington, nearly four months later. Come to that, there is a lot that we can be pretty certain that Alfred really did. He does not appear on the historical stage in a puff of smoke: there is plenty of material to set him in historical context. Why not concentrate on all those things?

Alfred's wars with the Vikings, his eventual triumph and subsequent innovations have long been seen as a high point in Anglo-Saxon history, and the various contemporary accounts of it a shaft of light on the Dark Ages that followed the departure of the Romans at the beginning of the fifth century and lasted, in traditional versions, until the Norman Conquest of 1066. By Alfred's time, the ninth century, several of the smaller kingdoms of Anglo-Saxon England had been assimilated into the four remaining realms of Northumbria to the north, East Anglia in the east, Mercia in the midlands and Wessex in the west. At different times in the preceding centuries, different kingdoms had been pre-eminent – Mercia, for example, was the most powerful in the eighth century, under King Aethelbald, then King Offa.

Wessex had established itself as the strongest Anglo-Saxon kingdom under Alfred's grandfather Egbert, who had defeated both Mercian and Northumbrian forces, though he had not achieved, or perhaps attempted, outright conquest. While Mercia and Northumbria regained or retained independent status, it looks as though Wessex continued as the most powerful kingdom under Alfred's father, Aethelwulf. It was he who had first to contend with the escalation of attacks from the Scandinavian pirates and (later) would-be conquerors known as the Vikings. Alfred's successes afterwards have all but erased the fact of his father's triumph in what sounds like one of the largest battles of the age, when he defeated a substantial Viking force at the now unknown site of Aclea in 851. Four years later he apparently felt secure enough from threat to undertake a pilgrimage to Rome, a journey

2. A gold and niello ring inscribed with King Aethelwulf, Alfred's father's name. It may have been given to a follower rather than belonging to the king himself. Alfred's grandson would be praised by the Anglo-Saxon Chronicle as a 'ring-giver'.

he combined with the sealing of his second marriage, to one of the most eligible women in Europe: a Frankish princess, the great-granddaughter of Charlemagne. If Aethelwulf's sons – each of whom succeeded him in turn until Alfred, the youngest, inherited at the age of twenty-two – had to contend with an ever-increasing Viking threat, the achievements of their father and grandfather had ensured that it was a prosperous, settled and well-allied kingdom that they had to defend.

This, briefly, is the 'real' background to the romance of Alfred and the cakes. So do we really need to bother with fairy tales when there is such a lot of grown-up material to examine? One answer is that the Alfred of Chippenham and Edington, the son of an established ruling house, let alone the king who at different times fulfilled the roles of scholar, lawgiver, administrator and politician, has weathered so badly in comparison to the Alfred of the cakes. The story has kept his name alive in popular terms. In a BBC television poll in 2002 Alfred managed to get into the top twenty 'Greatest Britons', while the substance of his achievement has all but vanished from popular view. We can't be sure of the voters' reasons, but it seems unlikely that the respondents who voted for him were thinking 'victor of Edington' or 'organiser of the burghal system' rather than 'the one who burned the cakes', even if, long after its Victorian heyday, they would have struggled to recall the details of the story. But there is more to the argument than 'if you can't beat them, join them'.

What stories – especially ones as long-lasting, persistent and adaptable as the story of Alfred and the cakes – *can* tell us is how we and those who went before us came to see a period, or a person, in the way we do. In general, scholars only give stories and myths house room in order to contrast them with 'real' history. As one, Simon Keynes, has written (in a long essay that definitively draws together the strands of the king's cult over a millennium), 'only when we understand the circumstances in which received tradition developed can we begin to strip off and clear away the accumulation of preconceptions, assumptions and expectations which might otherwise affect how we formulate the questions that we ask of the available evidence'. Historians are used to separating fact from fantasy and dismissing the latter; but in the case of Alfred, a king who has been famous on and off for over a thousand years, fact and fantasy are inextricably bound together. Taking stories of various vintages and renown as a way into a discussion of the different aspects of his life and achievement helps to remind us that we are dealing with a myth as much as with a man.

It is extremely difficult to reach a consensus on the events even of the relatively recent past. When it comes to an age as distant as Alfred's, it is probably useless to pretend that we can access the past directly, applying rigorous standards of evidence like white spirit to the layers of myth, prejudice and interpretation that have built up over the centuries to reveal the unvarnished truth. The truth is lost. Astringent applications to what remains are more likely to wipe out the whole than reveal the original.

As for the story of Alfred and the cakes, both the tale itself and its longevity represent something, and that may be worth keeping. The reasons it was told in the first place, the reasons it survived and the reasons it was picked up and polished into what Winston Churchill described as one of the 'gleaming toys of history', all these are legitimate, in fact vital, concerns for understanding a moment in the distant past and what it has come to mean to us today. Historians are engaged in an act not of re-creation but of restoration. We can restore an old picture, speculate about the darker portions, but to do so while attempting to ignore the residue of previous restorations that remains on the canvas is to blind ourselves to the image we are faced with.

The story of the cakes, moreover, is only one aspect of an Alfred myth that grew up in the decades and centuries after his death. In the course of this book we will come across ideas that were at one time seriously advanced about Alfred but which now seem even more fanciful than the recurring (and appealing) notion of the king unrecognised in his own realm. And most, though not all, of the ingrained ideas about Alfred have stories attached to them – some written down in Alfred's own time; others, like the cakes, relatively shortly afterwards; others still originating hundreds of years later. These stories would be told by historians, embellished by novelists, re-imagined by painters or invoked by politicians. Some pieces of Alfrediana, such as the 'Rule Britannia' chorus from an eighteenth-century play called *Alfred: A Masque*, have taken on a life completely independent of the king who first inspired them and become part of the national identity of a nation Alfred wouldn't recognise. The reasons that one story endures while another is forgotten often have little to do with their likely historical accuracy. For example, in the classic high imperial work of children's British history *Our Island Story* (1905) the author, H. E. Marshall, for whom there was 'never a better king in England' than Alfred, includes most of the time-honoured Alfred stories, gathered indiscriminately from contemporary sources, later embellishments and pure wishful thinking. As well as the cakes, there are: the reading competition in which the young Alfred wins a 'beautifully coloured' book; the founding of the Royal Navy (Alfred achieves the 'first of many, many sea-victories which the English have won'); the capture of the Vikings' magical Raven Banner in battle; the king's disguise as a minstrel to gain access to the enemy's camp; the invention of the jury and the establishment of a peace so universal that 'golden chains and bracelets might be hung upon the hedges and no one would touch them'; and the invention of the candle clock, though not, surprisingly, Alfred as the first king of England. Marshall's Alfred is a model for British children: truth-telling, violent only when absolutely necessary, and standing at the head of a tradition of vigorous, naval-backed independence. And when Marshall's Alfred builds 'more great ships, and sen[ds] people into far countries to bring back news of them to England', while 'encourag[ing] the English to make all kinds of things, in order to trade with

3. Various elements of the historical and mythical Alfred are present in this eighteenth-century engraving: soldier's shield, bow and arrows, Christian cross, minstrel's lyre, captured Viking banner.

these far-off countries', the British empire, free trade and imperial tariff reform don't seem very far off.

Co-opting Alfred into a vision of a present-day political ideal did not die out at the turn of the twentieth century. *Our Island Story* was republished in 2005 after a campaign in which it was specifically invoked as an 'antidote to the fractured, incoherent history most primary school children are taught today'. Marshall's description of Alfred – 'truthful and fearless in everything ... England's Darling' – makes him a key representative of the heroic, nationalist and antimodern political vision that the campaign is attempting to promote. Equally well, more progressive views of the king, in which he is depicted as a master propagandist or protoEuropean, may also owe more to contemporary debate than their holders make out.

ALFRED'S SPECIAL CASE

The roots of the entanglement of Alfred's life and myth thus go very deep. It can be difficult to say exactly why one historical subject receives more attention than another and why the attention takes the form it does, but with Alfred, in very simple terms, it is possible to discern three main reasons, overlapping, but nevertheless distinct. The first is that, for an Anglo-Saxon king, a relatively large amount of contemporary or near contemporary material survives about him. There is a biography written in Latin by Asser, one of Alfred's bishops; there are the year-by-year historical accounts known as the Anglo-Saxon Chronicle, a compilation that Alfred himself, or his court, initiated; there are Alfred's own translations from Latin into Old English of religious and secular classics of the age, as well as those of his court circle; there is the king's will and his law code, as well as a smattering of charters, a peace treaty, a letter or two and an administrative document, the Burghal Hidage, that gives a picture of the defensive reforms enacted in Alfred's reign.

So historians have a lot to go on, at least for a ninth-century West Saxon king. There may even be a danger of believing implicitly in Alfred's importance, purely because more survives on parchment about him than about so many of his predecessors or successors (although that very survival may form part of an argument for his importance). The sources also need to be handled carefully because of their very nature. Asser's book is little short of hagiography, and its method and structure – particularly its insistence on a personal familiarity with its subject and its liberal use of stories – have affected the way we think about the king ever since; Alfred's own writings naturally present him in a flattering light, and most of the rest emerges from under the king's eyes, if not his pen.

This brings us to the second secret of Alfred's success: his personality. Crucially, thanks to Asser and Alfred's own writings, he has one. Asser's book may be partial, but it portrays a flesh-and-blood figure, sometimes too vividly for squeamish tastes (the details of the king's battle with piles might give even the most committed modern royal biographer pause). Asser's personal portrait of the king, as well as glimpses from his own writings, present a far more troubled, vulnerable figure than the confident public-school hero of subsequent versions. Alfred's own literary output is made up of translations, but he wrote some introductory matter and made enough personal amendments to give an insight into the way he saw the world. We may no longer take what

Alfred tells us, let alone what Asser says, at face value. So no modern historian will write of Alfred as a Victorian predecessor could, as 'the most perfect character in history'. But Alfred appears an appealingly intelligent, complex, remarkable man, and not just because we have been afforded a sight of him.

The third reason that Alfred gets so much attention is the misleadingly simple one that he is 'great'. This may sound unfair to modern scholars, who certainly qualify their assessments of him far more carefully than their predecessors of a hundred or so years ago. But, for all their scrupulousness, recent major biographies and collections of primary material make their first 'a-historical' move by referring in their titles to Alfred 'the Great'. Yet the same authors will freely admit that there is no evidence that Alfred was called 'the Great' in his own time or even immediately after it. In fact, it was not until the thirteenth century that the epithet gets its first known outing (in Matthew Paris's *History of the Abbots of St Albans*, written before 1259), and not until at least 300 years later that it really stuck.

Alfred's 'greatness', in name and reputation, was not a foregone conclusion, and it was thrust upon him only gradually in the centuries after his death. For the year he died, 899, the Anglo-Saxon Chronicle gave him no special encomium. In the eleventh century Aelfric, the star of Anglo-Saxon letters, made Alfred only one of three Anglo-Saxon kings 'often victorious through God'. Of Alfred's Anglo-Saxon successors, one alone – Aethelred ('the Unready') – used his name for a son (his eighth and youngest), whereas other previous incumbents' names were all recycled (though it is conceivable that this absence is more a compliment than a sign of neglect, that Alfred's name was 'retired', like a famous football player's shirt number). By the same measure Alfred's later reputation took a long time to revive: until 1780, to be precise, when the ninth and youngest son of George III was named Alfred: he died in his second year.

It might be legitimately argued that Alfred's nickname is now as much a part of him as Charlemagne's much older one (his epitaph already made him 'magnus') is of him. It no more carries a value judgement than a modern surname; it merely identifies him. But modern historians don't just call Alfred 'great'; they treat him as great too, although the greatness will be wrestled with and redefined. Sometimes they seem reluctant, but they tend to give in. Alfred's most recent biographer, Richard Abels, writes of being 'resistant to the idea of Alfred's "greatness"', but eventually succumbing to it, while emphasising that it was the 'greatness of a Dark Age king' rather than that of a Victorian-style paragon. Similarly, Alfred P. Smyth, the author of a monumental biography that is so distrustful of myth-making that it rejects the authenticity of Asser (reviving a popular parlour game in which modern Anglo-Saxon historians attempt to make things difficult for themselves by chucking out the best contemporary source for Alfred's life), still ends up at a version of the great king, whose 'true genius ... was his ability not so much to excel, as to possess the qualities of an all-rounder'. Are we so very far away from the Victorian verdict that 'No other man on record has ever so thoroughly united all the virtues both of the ruler and of the private man'?

The author of that judgement, the Whiggish scholar and populariser E. A. Freeman, was quite aware that Alfred was an 'instance of a prince who has become the hero of romance', but it was his view that the romance might actually reflect something of the truth. Despite the 'countless imaginary exploits and imaginary institutions attributed to him', he wrote, Alfred 'appears in exactly the same light in history and fable'. We may want to refine that, and Freeman's proto-imperial Alfred certainly reads like the creation of the nineteenth century rather than the ninth – a part of the myth built up by historians rather than storytellers. But even if later historians are more cautious in their statements, those statements arise of necessity from informed speculation based on skewed and incomplete sources, which, from the beginning, present a mythical Alfred as much as a genuine one. To illustrate the point we need make only a very simple comparison.

Alfred's successors were his son Edward the Elder and grandson Aethelstan. Their achievements – what is known of them – in some respects arguably outweigh those of their father and grandfather. Edward, a gifted general, did not merely hold off the Vikings, as Alfred did. He began the expansion of Wessex into the midland former kingdom of Mercia, which the Vikings had settled as part of what became known as the 'Danelaw' after their defeat by Alfred. Edward's military and diplomatic operation is often called the 'reconquest of the Danelaw', although as the territory had never belonged to the West Saxons, 'conquest' is more accurate. Edward's son Aethelstan is the first credible holder of a title once wishfully foisted on Alfred, king of England. There is not a great deal of surviving source material about Edward, but for Aethelstan there are vestiges of a Life written in Latin, drawn on by William of Malmesbury in the twelfth century, no fewer than six law codes, as well as the record of the Chronicle, including a famous poem detailing Aethelstan's triumph at the Battle of Brunanburh (937), when, at a now unknown location, he defeated an army combining the forces of the Viking king of Dublin and the kings of the Scots and of Strathclyde.

Of the three – Alfred, Edward and Aethelstan – only grandson Aethelstan comes in for special treatment by the Chronicle, which describes him as 'lord of nobles, dispenser of treasure to men'. Yet, for all Edward and his son's achievements and, in Aethelstan's case at least, the existence of a reasonable amount of source material, neither king is anything like as closely studied as Alfred. It is not, I am sure, unconnected that neither has ever been even remotely as well known to the public – that is, that their myth, as much as their history, has been neglected. We have never been told that they 'burned the cakes' or 'founded the Navy' or 'stole into the enemy's camp dressed as a minstrel'. Only Alfred did all that, at least in some versions of his story.

So it is important at the outset to admit that Alfred's fame may not rest purely on his various accomplishments or his unique character, no matter how remarkable these were. It rests on some accidents of literary survival. And a part of that survival consists of the legends and stories that began with his first biographer, Asser, and were adapted and added to in the succeeding centuries. These legends and stories are so intrinsic to Alfred's historical make-up that they offer an alternative way of beginning to look at him, of putting him in context and of understanding how he is as much the repository as the origin of so many of our most deeply held ideas about his age, and about England. By starting out with Alfred's stories I hope to show how impressions of his life and reputation crystallised in some cases or altered and vanished from view in others. Rather than scrubbing away layers of varnish, we can take a step back and attempt to view the whole picture for what it is: beguiling and intriguing but admittedly artificial.

In the course of this stepping back we may learn something about not just Alfred and ninth-century England but also about the way history is recast in different ages and places. Why do some stories last while others fade away? Some are very particular to their own historical and geographical context. So Alfred becomes the founder of a university or the fount of local government practices. Others have an almost universal appeal, which is more the case with the story of the cakes, where the unrecognised king goes among his people, a theme explored from King David in the Bible to the duke in *Measure for Measure*, from the Brothers Grimm (the Frog Prince) to the *Ramayana* (where the Lord Rama goes into forest exile, much like Alfred).

The first person to write at length about Alfred, his biographer Asser, knew that the stories he told about him were likely to fix his subject in our minds. To a modern reader Asser is frustratingly full of gaps. He forgets to tell us the name of Alfred's wife, for example, apparently because he is too eager to get to a story about the king's mother-in-law, whose name he does remember to include. But the stories that Asser tells stay with the reader; they also inspired other generations to add their own elaborations, creating the composite Alfred that we have today. It is this Alfred, rather than the vanishing 'real' one, that we will meet in this book.

1

THE PROMISED BOOK AND THE
PILGRIM: ALFRED'S CHILDHOOD

The story of Alfred and the cakes describes a king unrecognised in his own land. But in some ways it is surprising that Alfred was king at all. He was the youngest of
five sons and one daughter and cannot have expected, or
have been expected, to succeed to the throne of Wessex.
Admittedly, most Anglo-Saxon dynasties were not secure
enough for their rules of succession to be rigid. Alfred's
father, Aethelwulf, was the first West Saxon king to succeed
his own father in almost 200 years. It has been suggested
that Aethelwulf intended to divide his kingdom equally
between his remaining sons, as Frankish kings did. But that
would have necessitated living longer, and in more peaceful
circumstances. In the event, Aethelwulf was succeeded by
his eldest surviving son. The immediate military threat from
the Vikings, however, meant that there was no time to wait
for a child heir to grow up, so as each of Aethelwulf's sons
died, the next brother inherited. If any of Alfred's brothers
had lived long enough to produce a mature son to succeed,
Alfred would surely have been passed over. As we shall see,
the survival of his last brother's two sons with a legitimate
claim would cause problems after Alfred's death.

For Asser, the Welsh bishop who attended his court and

wrote his Life, Alfred's initial distance from the throne was a problem. He needed to show that his man was fated to be king anyway. Later Alfred would be made to embody a variety of destinies, from the spirit of England to the incarnation of Empire. But the process of establishing Alfred as a man of destiny started, as with so many ideas about the king, with Asser. One way in which he did this was to give the reader a glimpse of Alfred as a boy. Because of Asser's biography, Alfred is the first Anglo-Saxon king, perhaps the first Anglo-Saxon, whom it is possible to imagine as a child. The picture Asser offers of Alfred's childhood includes one of the most indelible of all Alfred's stories, and one that, despite its many problems, has become an adaptably secure part of Alfred's myth:

> One day, therefore, when his mother was showing him and his brothers a book of English poetry which she held in her hand, she said: 'I shall give this book to whichever one of you can learn it the fastest.' Spurred on by these words, or rather by divine inspiration, and attracted by the beauty of the initial letter of the book, Alfred spoke as follows in reply to his mother, forestalling his brothers (ahead in years, though not in ability): 'Will you really give this book to the one of us who can understand it the soonest and recite it to you?' Whereupon, smiling with pleasure, she reassured him, saying: 'Yes I will.' He immediately took the book from her hand, went to his teacher and learned it. When it was learned, he took it back to his mother and recited it.

From our first personal encounter with Alfred he is made special, different from his brothers, who are 'ahead in years,

though not in ability'. Unsurprisingly, Asser is the only contemporary source for such a personal and intimate picture
of his subject's childhood: no other account can corroborate
it. The details are so vague that it reads like an exemplary
tale, and in some respects this is the best way to view it. In
later versions of the story some of the missing details will be
imaginatively supplied, and Alfred's closeness to his mother,
or the inspiration he takes from the material in the book, will
emerge as the dominant motifs. But Asser is making a different set of points, about Alfred's destiny to be king and the
sort of king he is destined to be.

Alfred's early years are a problem for Asser not only
because he clearly felt that he should demonstrate how the
boy was a king-in-waiting. He cannot boast for this period,
as he does at other times in his book, that 'I have seen for
myself with my own eyes' the things or events he describes.
Asser didn't arrive at Alfred's court until the king was an
adult, and for such a personal story of Alfred's childhood as
the promised book the only likely surviving witness must
have been Alfred himself. So Asser, writing around 893
about events almost forty years earlier, is more than ever his
master's mouthpiece for this story.

The story of Alfred's triumph over his older brothers in
the book competition is of a piece with the rest of Asser's
picture of Alfred as a boy. He tells us that Alfred 'was greatly
loved, more than all his brothers, by his father and mother
– indeed, by everybody', and that he 'was always brought
up in the royal court and nowhere else'. And though Asser
later praises Alfred's skills on the battlefield and in the
hunt, he identifies two themes in his master's childhood
to which he returns throughout his work, and which have
become an intrinsic part of the way we view the king. One

is his godliness, of which more later. The other emerges in a stronger way in the story of the promised book. It is Alfred's attachment to learning, and specifically to 'wisdom': 'From the cradle onwards, in spite of all the demands of the present life, it has been the desire for wisdom, more than anything else, together with the nobility of his birth, which have characterised the nature of his noble mind.' Asser's Alfred is from the beginning a learned, or would-be learned, king. His early life is seen as a preparation, not for the great contest against the Vikings who invaded his land and drove him into hiding, but for his later commitment to the spread of literacy and knowledge once victory had been secured.

ASSER, THE PIONEER

The inseparability of Alfred the man and Alfred the myth begins here, with Asser and with the first account of his childhood. Much of Asser's biography simply reproduces the entries of the Anglo-Saxon Chronicle for individual years. But Asser also wanted to leave a more individual account. He allows readers to see him struggling to impose a personal take on his material, apologising early on for his tendency to digress 'among such terrible wars and in year-by-year reckoning'. Asser has got to Alfred's eighteenth year, plunged the reader into accounts of Viking attacks on his father's kingdom, given details of a rebellion and settled down to tell us at length the story behind the West Saxons' reluctance to grant their queens the honour of sitting beside their husbands on the throne before he remembers that the idea behind his biography is to give an impression of the formation of his subject's character. 'I should no longer veer off course', he admonishes himself, and pledges to 'return to that which particularly inspired me to this work: in other words … some small account … of the infancy and boyhood of my esteemed lord Alfred'. It is at this point that Asser tells the story of the promised book, for which the Chronicle, concentrating on bloodier details of the adult world, has no place.

These more intimate touches are what gives Asser's work its abiding interest, but they also account for an unjustifiable tendency among later observers to imagine that they really 'know' Alfred, when in fact they know one man's version of him. And there are good general grounds for treating Asser cautiously; not because his work is a forgery, as some historians have argued (a debate to which we will return later, in Chapter 7), but for entirely understandable reasons to do with the time Asser was writing and with his own peculiarities.

To begin with, there is the question of bias. A contemporary and intimate of the king was no more likely to write an unbiased account of his still living subject in ninth-century Wessex than is a royal biographer today. Asser's account of Alfred reads more like a hagiography than anything a modern reader would call a biography. It puts a positive spin on almost every aspect of its subject's life and often tips over into sycophancy, as when Asser chastises himself for even suggesting a comparison, though an entirely innocent one, between Alfred and the good thief who was crucified with Christ – in case anyone should get the wrong idea and think Asser is criticising his master.

The structure of the book can also be hard to follow. At times it seems as if there are more gaps and elisions in it than there is reliable factual content. It also ends rather suddenly, recording nothing beyond the year 893, despite the fact that

Asser outlived his master; it has been suggested that the text we have is a first draft, rather than the finished article. Asser does not seem to us a natural biographer, or even a particularly gifted writer. His work has lasted because of its subject, not for its intrinsic merit. But part of the reason for these shortcomings is that Asser was writing in a barely formed genre: the biography of a layman, and of one who was likely to read the result. Though Asser himself had read precursors such as Einhard's Life of Charlemagne and probably a Life of the abbot Alcuin (of York, but who spent much of his career on the Continent, some of it in Charlemagne's court), he had no comparable royal models for his own island. There had been Lives of early English saints, men such as Cuthbert, Boniface and Wilfrid, though it isn't known for sure if Asser had read them. What we can be sure of is that Asser was in many ways as much a pioneer as his subject, and his apparent forgetfulness or difficulty with keeping focus may have as much to do with the newness of what he was attempting as with his personal failings.

This first version of Alfred's story, like every subsequent one down the centuries, is coloured by the character of the person who wrote it and by the people he wrote it for. So who was Asser? He tells us much of what we know. He was a Welsh monk whom Alfred invited to join him in his court for six months of each year so that 'the latter would derive benefit in every respect from the learning of St David, to the best of my abilities at least'. The timing of Asser's arrival can't be pinpointed, but the king was in his late thirties and had already been on the throne for about fourteen years. Asser was eventually made bishop of Sherborne, and it is possible that he was already a bishop, of St David's, when he met Alfred, though he himself is unclear on that, as on

so much else. At Alfred's court Asser joined a team of scholars assembled by his master to encourage the king's and his
subjects' education. It is possible too, of course, that Alfred
wanted Asser by him as his official biographer, but Asser
does not tell us so.

As for the people Asser wrote for: his first intended
reader, and the book's dedicatee, was his subject. His work
begins: 'To my esteemed and most holy lord, Alfred, ruler of
all the Christians of the island of Britain, King of the Angles
and Saxons, Asser, lowest of all the servants of God, wishes
thousandfold prosperity in this life and the next, according
to the desires of his prayers.' It has further been argued that
Asser's book was intended for the edification of Alfred's
courtiers, and particularly his own sons and potential heirs.
But Asser was also writing for the folks back home. He often
refers to the Welsh name of an English place, and it has been
proposed that one purpose of Asser's work was 'to reassure
the Welsh that they had submitted themselves to a wise and
Christian king'. So when reading Asser, it pays to keep in
mind not only that this was an authorised biography by a
first-time author, but also that it was directed beyond that to
an audience unfamiliar with an Anglo-Saxon court.

A STRANGE COMPETITION

Both the details (or lack of them) and the generalities of the
story of the promised book illustrate all this. Asser's vignette
of Alfred's childhood raises, first of all, some straightforward questions. When did this happen? What else do we
know about Alfred's mother? Or his brothers? Who was the
teacher to whom Alfred took the book? And considering how
thoroughly Alfred later lamented the decline of learning in

4. The opening lines of Asser's Life of Alfred, from a manuscript dated c1000. This facsimile was published in 1722. Nine years later, the manuscript on which it was based, the only such source for Asser's text, was destroyed in a fire.

his kingdom, the promised book itself prompts a few questions. What was in it, and what might it have looked like? Lastly, the very nature of the contest is, on closer inspection, a bit puzzling. Alfred's mother says she will give the book to 'whichever one of you can learn it the fastest', and Alfred checks the rules: 'Will you really give this book to the one of us who can understand it soonest and recite it to you?' he asks. Now Asser means to show that the prince's diligence and enthusiasm win him the book, but Alfred's next action surely guarantees success, or at least ensures that his brothers can't win. 'He immediately took the book from her hand, went to his teacher and learned it.' The others don't get a look-in. Where Asser sees honest enthusiasm, we might also see the planning and cunning that would prove to be two great virtues of his kingship; or, of course, a symptomatic vagueness about details in the approach of the biographer.

Asser tells us two things about the prize in the competition: the book. It is a book of 'English poetry', and it is illuminated with a beautiful 'initial letter'. Most of the Anglo-Saxon vernacular poetry that survives to this day is religious in content (the chief exception being *Beowulf*), but it is, of course, impossible to know what kind of poetry was in the book that Alfred won. It is worth noticing, however, that, despite the later descriptions of the decline, and almost extinction, of literacy and learning in Alfred's kingdom – which, Alfred himself claimed, pre-dated the Viking raids – books were common enough at the royal court for one to be entrusted to a child (albeit the paragon of Asser's creation). When Asser describes the book as containing 'English poetry', we are likely to think 'as against Latin', the only other language in which Anglo-Saxon literature (including Asser's own book) was written. But here might also be a moment where Asser is speaking to his Welsh audience, who would have preconceived ideas of what English, as against Welsh, poetry was like.

The answer to the question of when the contest happened may help us to decide how seriously to take the story. It has been calculated that Alfred's oldest brother was roughly twenty-four years his senior, and died about the time Alfred was at most five years old, so he is unlikely to have been part of this story. Even Alfred's own birth date, which Asser gives as 849, is disputed, so it is unsurprising that his less famous siblings are still more difficult to date. But charter evidence and informed guesswork have suggested that Alfred's next two brothers were about twelve and ten years older than him, that his sister was also around ten years older, while the fourth brother, Aethelred, may have been much closer to him in years. So it is tempting to argue that only one brother, Aethelred, was likely to have been part of the contest, and Asser is exaggerating the competition by referring to Alfred 'and his brothers' being shown the book by their mother.

Turning to the subject of Alfred's mother, however, may change that conclusion. Asser tells us that Alfred's mother was called Osburh, but he also tells us that after Alfred's father, Aethelwulf (with Alfred in tow), visited the Frankish court of Charles the Bald, on his way back from Rome in 855, he 'returned to his homeland, bringing with him Judith, daughter of Charles', as his wife. So Osburh must have been dead by the time Alfred was six. This means that the latest that the contest can be dated is when Alfred was around five years old, and his middle brother about fifteen. So if the story is taken at face value, and it is already becoming a bigger 'if', Anglo-Saxon princes were treated as children for rather longer than we might expect, and Alfred must have been a particularly precocious five-year-old.

As for the other details of the story, they are more tantalising than informative. The fact that Alfred had a teacher at all seems to contradict what Asser has him say later in life about his education: 'among all the difficulties and burdens of his present life this had become the greatest: namely, that at the time when he was of the right age and had the leisure and the capacity for learning, he did not have the teachers.' Clearly the person who coached the very young Alfred to win the book could not help him much further. In fact, Asser is unclear throughout his work about the state of Alfred's literacy. In the chapter before the story of the promised book he declares that 'by the shameful negligence of his parents and tutors he remained ignorant of letters until his twelfth year', well after the contest. Later Asser says of the adult Alfred that he 'had not yet begun to read anything' and again, a few chapters further on, that on a single day at the age of thirty-nine, Alfred 'first began through divine inspiration to read and to translate at the same time'. Unless Asser is to be completely dismissed as a fantasist or a forger, the last two statements should be interpreted as applying to the reading and comprehension of Latin. If the competition story has any factual basis, it is more a story about memorising than actual reading. Asser, of course, does not say whether Alfred's older siblings received a different or a better education, but the picture of the learned and diligent king-in-waiting has to be leavened a little with Asser's own admissions of his subject's scholarly frailties later in life.

Asser's intentions in telling the story seem fairly clear. He wanted to illustrate how the young Alfred was already marked out to be the Solomonic figure of his destiny. But subsequent versions of the story indicate a different set of interpretations, which account for its continuing popularity in a way that may have nothing to do with the historical Alfred or, we should say, the Alfred of his own and Asser's invention. This is a pattern that will be repeated throughout Alfred's history, as an early account becomes transmuted over the years into something very different, adding yet more aspects to the king's reputation while distancing us ever further from any idea of the 'true' picture. The alteration can come as much from a change in emphasis as the adding of details. In the case of the story of the promised book it is a tale that, unsurprisingly, has appealed to children, or at least to those writing for children, to show how a great hero must also be a model pupil.

Children's history matters when dealing with the formation of a historical myth: first impressions are as important in history as in daily life. Early convictions about the past take root in childhood reading, however unconsciously, in a way that can prove difficult to dislodge. Here is the children's historian R. J. Unstead with a fairly representative version of the story, first published in *People in History* in 1957:

One day the Queen was sitting in the Great Hall, and she called her four sons to her:

'What is this I am holding, my sons?'

'It is a book, Mother,' answered the eldest, Ethelbald.

'Yes, it is a book of Saxon poetry. Which of you can read it to me?'

'Reading is for monks. We learn to hunt and to fight the Northmen. Letters take too long to learn.'

'But, my son,' said the Queen, 'I want you to learn your letters. A prince who cannot read will make a sorry king. I will give this book to the one who first learns to read it.'

Alfred pushed between his brothers and looked at the beautiful writing, copied by monks, and at the great letter which stood at the top of the page, painted in glowing colours. He longed to have the book for his own.

'Will you really give me this book, Mother, if I can read it to you?' he asked.

'Yes, Alfred,' answered the Queen. 'If you can read it before your brothers, it shall be yours to keep.'

The four princes began to learn their letters, in the hope of winning the beautiful book. They found it dull work, and soon three of them went off to practise shooting with a bow, and fighting with battle-axes. But Alfred went to the abbey and asked the monk who had taught him parts of the Bible if he would teach him to read. He worked every day at his reading lessons, until at last he was able to read the book of Saxon poetry, and to claim it from his mother.

In this version we are presented with Alfred as a member of an idealised family (including his second eldest brother, Aethelbald, who perhaps a year later would be running the kingdom in his father's absence, rebelling against him and generally being a bit too grown up to have taken part so recently in the family reading lesson). Unstead makes the competition specifically about reading rather than memorising, and goes even further than Asser in emphasising Alfred's early preference for scholarly diligence over 'fighting with battle-axes'. But other details have not altered radically from Asser's 'original'. The book and Alfred's superiority to his brothers are still the focus of the story, as they are for Asser, but the figure of Osburh, Alfred's mother, is fleshed out a little, and any sense that Asser gives of the 'shameful negligence' of his parents in not teaching him better is replaced by a loving idyll. By the time Unstead wrote, it was only in children's history that such an idealised popular picture would appear. What had begun with Asser, been refined over the

5. Alfred's nuclear family, as pictured in a twentieth-century children's book.

centuries and reached its apogee in the nineteenth century –
the portrayal of Alfred as 'the ideal Englishman' – had in the
twentieth century been much diluted. Academic historians
had more soberly pronounced on Asser's book, with some
even doubting its genuineness. But even popular reimagin-
ings of Alfred's story, when directed towards adults, were
less idealised. In Alfred Duggan's novel *The King of Athelney*
(1961) Alfred is shown getting around the rules of the contest

rather than winning it by 'divine inspiration'. Duggan has Osburh 'dropping in' on her sons' lessons, rather than being the focus of them. The idea of Alfred at the heart of a perfect family is best seen as (mostly Victorian) embellishment.

In children's history, pictures are at least as important as words. In R. J. Unstead or the Ladybird Alfred of similar vintage the prince is pictured with his (far too young) brothers gathered in a scene of rather later medieval family bliss. Just as the children's historians are writing in a Victorian tradition that follows precursors such as Thomas Hughes (of *Tom Brown's Schooldays*) – who wrote a life of Alfred, 'the typical English King', for the 'Sunday Library for Household Reading' in 1869 – so the illustrators have their own nineteenth-century antecedents. The ideals portrayed in Asser prove to be even more elastic in artists' hands, especially if they get hung up on attempting 'factual' accuracy. So Richard Westall's painting of *The Boyhood of King Alfred*, at the end of the eighteenth century, showed a rather older prince at his mother and father's knee, with a monk–teacher standing behind. But, as the painting's alternative title, *Queen Judith Reciting to Alfred the Great, When a Child, the Songs of the Bards, Describing the Heroic Deeds of his Ancestors*, illustrates, Westall had an unusual take on the story. Judith was Alfred's stepmother, and here the painter was following a tradition introduced by the twelfth-century historian William of Malmesbury, who understood Asser to mean that Alfred learned any form of literacy at the age of twelve (a perfectly reasonable interpretation of Asser's words), and so had his stepmother set the competition. Less historically specific is Alfred Stevens's later, idealised *King Alfred and his Mother* (1848), which can be seen in Tate Britain. In it, a Quattrocento Alfred and Madonna-like Osburh gaze into each other's

6. *A re-enactment of the reading competition from the Alfred millenary at Winchester, 1901.*

eyes, their hands placed on the book that is his destiny. These paintings exclude Alfred's brothers to concentrate on his relationship with his mother and often to emphasise that the poems being read describe the 'heroic deeds of his ancestors'. What begins in Asser as a story marking out the young prince as a future scholar and a special individual, destined to be king, has become by turns a picture of motherly love, Victorian domesticity and an explicit foreshadowing of Alfred's own 'heroic' martial deeds.

A PAPAL AUDIENCE

Far less common as a subject for either painters or popular historians is a much more remarkable story from Alfred's childhood also told by Asser and, unlike the story of the book, corroborated in part by the Chronicle and other sources. In 853 and 855, Asser tells us, at the age of four and then six, Alfred travelled to Rome, the first time without his family, the second accompanied by his father. On the first occasion Asser writes that Pope Leo IV 'anointed the child Alfred as king, ordaining him properly, received him as an adoptive son and confirmed him'. The second time Alfred's father took his youngest 'because he loved him more than his other sons' and stayed for a year, stopping off on his return at the court of Charles the Bald, the Frankish king, where he collected Charles's daughter Judith to be his new wife. (Asser hasn't told us that Aethelwulf's first wife is dead, but we surmise that she must have died before he left.) The story is so unlikely in so many respects – Alfred undergoing the arduous trip to Rome as a child not once but twice, unaccompanied by his family the first time; the papal 'anointment' as king of a four-year-old child whose claim to the throne was extremely tenuous at the time – that it is tempting to dismiss it entirely. But there are good reasons to believe that this, or something like this, is what really happened, in contrast to the book story.

Asser often merely reproduces the entry in the Anglo-Saxon Chronicle for a certain year, but in the case of Alfred's pilgrimage to Rome he varies it a little. The Chronicle only records one visit to Rome – the first one, unaccompanied by his father – whereas Asser very definitely records two. Most scholars agree that if Alfred authorised Asser's biography of him, his influence on the Chronicle was hardly less direct. So the fact that these two sources overlap is hardly convincing proof of Alfred's visit, and the fact that they disagree over the details merely clouds the issue further. But there is a fragment of a letter sent by the pope, Leo IV, to Alfred's father, preserved in a twelfth-century collection. It seems to corroborate at least one of Alfred's visits, surprisingly the one without his father (that is, the one in the Chronicle):

> To Aethelwulf, king of the English. We have now graciously received your son Alfred, whom you were anxious to send at this time to the thresholds of the Holy Apostles, and we have decorated him, as a spiritual son, with the dignity of the sword and the vestments of the consulate, as is customary with Roman consuls, because he gave himself into our hands.

Though some doubt has been cast on the authenticity of this letter (its preservation in the later form means it can't be proved to date from the ninth century), it is now generally accepted. The ceremony it describes is, of course, rather different from the royal anointing of Asser and the Chronicle. Only generosity to Alfred can save him from the charge that he at least embellished this story in later years to fit his own sense of destiny. One biographer, Richard Abels, has intriguingly suggested that Alfred's model for this may have been King David, who was marked out by Samuel as above his brothers. Certainly such an example would have appealed to Alfred, who later translated the Psalms. And if Alfred did manipulate the story for its propaganda potential, it is instructive to see at work the sophistication of a king popularly seen as the straightest of arrows.

Whatever the reality of Alfred's visit, it is puzzling that it has not become as secure a part of Alfred's story as so many other episodes. Scholars' doubts about the details, and hesitations over the possibility that Alfred was in some degree responsible for falsifying the record of what happened in

Rome, together with the frustrating fact that the influence of a Roman visit on such a young boy cannot have been very great, may all contribute to its relatively minor part in most retellings of Alfred's life. But it does seem odd that such a colourful episode should not form a more memorable part of his legend. There is only one painting of the scene (again by Westall, and in entitling his painting *Prince Alfred before Pope Leo III*, rather than Leo IV, again showing that artist's distinct take on history), and no children's account mentions this extraordinary trip. Alfred Duggan's novel is an exception, treating it at length and taking the inspiration of Rome's faded but still impressive splendour as significant in Alfred's later life. But why has Rome otherwise disappeared from the popular Alfred, while the promised book and other stories remain? One reason may be that a moral adaptable beyond Alfred's own circumstances is not so easy to extract. In fact, the very specifics of the story may account for its relative obscurity.

Perhaps the most likely explanation for the story's popular demise, however, is to be found in Anglo-papal relations in later centuries. The beginnings of the recovery of the Anglo-Saxon past from contemporary manuscripts, such as Asser's book and the Chronicle, happened to coincide with the birth pangs of the Anglican Church. Asser's first editor, Elizabeth I's Archbishop Matthew Parker, whose name is also associated with one recension of the Anglo-Saxon Chronicle, used his researches to publish a book entitled *De Antiquitate Britannicae Ecclesiae* in 1572. Alfred's contribution later in life to revitalising the Church through his scholarly programmes, as well as his foundation of various religious houses, made him for Parker and his followers a vital part of the Church of England's antiquity and individuality. It was an article of faith to them that, as a contemporary bishop put it, 'we have planted no new religion, but only have renewed the old'.

But Alfred's efforts to reanimate his native Church were of a piece with his dedication to its papal overlord. Alfred and his family were committed to Rome – they regularly sent alms there and, according to Asser, received from the pope a piece of the True Cross. Their pride in this special relationship was, however, passed over at the time of Alfred's 'rediscovery' by historians, and the neglect became habitual. So, right at the beginning of Alfred's story, we are dealing not just with the contemporary biases and confusions of those who first wrote his life, or with the king's own remoulding of his past, but with the accretion over centuries of other influences. So the morally instructive story of the promised book remains a favourite, while a pope's faintly embarrassing seal of approval is politely ignored. Neither is in any verifiable sense a picture of the 'real' Alfred, but one has seemed more acceptable than the other.

2

BIRDS OF PREY: THE VIKINGS

The stories of studiousness and religious devotion from Alfred's childhood give us an idealised picture of the future king at peace. For most of his life, however, Alfred and his family were at war. The Vikings – the people he fought against, suffered defeat against, and defeated in turn – defined him. Alfred's achievement has always been seen as something beyond mere feats of arms, but without them, and without the Vikings, he would not be remembered for anything else.

Accounts of the period call Alfred's lifelong foe by different names – heathens, pagans, Northmen, Norse, Danes and Vikings (which is thought simply to mean 'pirate' and is the term preferred here, because it does not restrict the geographical origins of men and women who came from across Scandinavia). These formidable fighters pose problems for the historian, but to the storyteller and myth-maker they have proved irresistible. Pre-Christian Scandinavians were not, contrary to popular belief, illiterate: evidence of their runic script survives in almost every territory they inhabited. But these runic survivals, carved on stones and artefacts for practical and ritual purposes, do not provide anything like a joined-up narrative of their deeds. When looking at the Vikings, therefore, we must always bear in mind that the pagan invaders of Alfred's time and earlier did not write their own history. What they left behind is a combination of the accidents of archaeology, the reports of their enemies in England, Frankia and Ireland, and the records of oral tradition and plain invention created much later in the Scandinavian sagas and histories of the twelfth and thirteenth centuries. They have, over a thousand years and more, been variously portrayed as murderous savages, misunderstood traders, religious fanatics or, conversely, opportunists for whom any religion was just a flag of convenience.

The earliest accounts of the war between the Vikings and Anglo-Saxons, however, are clear in presenting it as a war of religions. One of the first Viking raids on England reported in detail by the Anglo-Saxon Chronicle took place just over fifty years before Alfred's birth, when the monastery of Lindisfarne in Northumbria was attacked in 793. The Chronicle was actually a compilation of different sets of annals, first made in Alfred's reign but incorporating material from different sources, written in different locations. Like almost all such accounts across Europe, these chronicles were almost exclusively the work of churchmen, monks whose picture of the outside world reflects the preoccupations of their own religious communities. It is the 'northern' version of the Anglo-Saxon Chronicle that gives an appropriately apocalyptic flavour to the arrival of the pagan attackers:

In this year, dire portents appeared over Northumbria. They consisted of immense whirlwinds and flashes of lightning, and fiery dragons were seen flying in the air. A great famine followed, and a little after that, on 8 June, the ravages of heathen men miserably destroyed God's church on Lindisfarne.

As we shall see, the Vikings' 'heathenism', their pagan otherness, flagged up by Christian observers with the most to lose from their depredations, was long seen as their identifying feature. And the religious overtones of their attacks were invoked from the beginning. The expatriate Northumbrian Alcuin wrote from the Carolingian court to his former fellows at Lindisfarne that 'this indeed has not happened by chance; it is a sign that someone has well deserved it'. He asked, 'What can we say except weep with you in our hearts before the altar of Christ and say, "Spare thy people O Lord and give not thine heritage to the Gentiles lest the heathens should say, 'Where is the God of the Christians?'"?' And quoting the same passage of scripture that would later be cited in connection with Alfred's lowest ebb and the story of the cakes, Hebrews 12:6, he reminded his correspondents: 'God chasteneth every son whom he receiveth.' In the preface to one of his translations Alfred himself described the Vikings' ravages as 'punishments'.

The Vikings were a divine judgement, but they could also be people to do business with. The main text of the Chronicle reports, at an unspecified time around the turn of the eighth century, the first Viking attack on Wessex. A local reeve (a royal official) was killed as he went to meet the 'first ships of Danish men which came to the land of the English', in Portland in Dorset. The reeve appeared to think that the men had come to trade. Much has been made by archaeologists and more recent historians of the more sophisticated aspects of Viking society. We only need to look at the most obvious product of their skill, the Viking longship, to understand how capable they were, not only as individual engineers but as members of a society able to organise itself to produce such magnificent ships (and their sails) on a grand scale. Though the numbers

7. The Gokstad Ship, built around 890 and excavated in Norway in 1880, was a triumph of engineering: a nineteenth-century replica crossed the Atlantic in twenty-eight days. Inset the picture shows the spoils of war: a silver hoard from Cuerdale, Lancashire, dating to just after Alfred's reign, and containing hundreds of coins with his name, now divided between the British and Ashmolean Museums.

given by Christian chroniclers have been doubted, fleets of sometimes hundreds of these ships are mentioned, which would involve technical feats of skill and organisation far beyond any 'primitive' society. The Vikings made brooches and skates, played board-games and built halls. They were by no means simple marauders. But as the ninth century wore on, any doubts about the long-term intentions of the attackers would be quelled. They may have been able traders, but the men who arrived in England were there for war.

THE SONS OF RAGNAR

In 865, when Alfred was about sixteen and his elder brother Aethelred had only recently succeeded as king of Wessex, the character of Viking attacks on England changed significantly. Previously the attackers had hit and run, plundering a quick profit before moving on. True, Viking expeditions had been known to spend the winter on English soil: only the previous year Aethelred's predecessor had been forced to buy off a band who had encamped on the isle of Thanet in Kent, though he hadn't secured their peaceful co-operation. But in 865 an invasion force arrived. Wessex was not initially under direct attack, but as events unfolded it would become clear that the Vikings had the whole of England in their sights. What the Chronicle calls a 'Great Heathen Army' landed in East Anglia and, after spending the winter there, was bought off by the East Anglians with horses, on which they headed north to Northumbria. There the Great Army occupied York and defeated a force combined by two rival Northumbrian kings, Aella and Osberht, who had eventually suppressed their differences to attack the city, in 867. The two kings were killed, either on the battlefield or later (and, as we shall see, perhaps more ritualistically), before the Vikings moved south. They attacked Mercia and occupied Nottingham. Despite teaming up with their West Saxon allies (including Prince Alfred), the Mercians were unable to force the Great Army into battle, and ended up 'making peace', as the Chronicle describes it, with the enemy (i.e., paying them off) to get rid of them, if only temporarily. If Mercia and its king, Burgred, were under any illusions about the efficacy of 'making peace' with the Vikings as a long-term strategy, they would have been disabused by what happened next. The Great Army returned to East Anglia, and this time the East Anglians did face them in battle. The third royal victim of the Army was Edmund, who died either fighting them or, again according to legend, in a more ritualised way after being taken prisoner. (Edmund was later canonised and memorialised in the name of the Suffolk town of Bury St Edmund.) Though the Vikings had installed a puppet ruler, Egbert, to oversee part of Northumbria, they took direct control of East Anglia, which ceased to exist as an independent kingdom. Mercia would not be spared, but the Army now turned its attentions towards Wessex, where Alfred's brother Aethelred was on the throne. The year was 871, and Alfred was in his early twenties. Already he had been on an inconclusive expedition to Mercia and seen at first hand what a formidable enemy he faced. Later that year he became king. The past five years would have taught him that anyone on the throne of Wessex was likely to be fighting not just to protect his kingdom but to save it and, most likely, to save himself.

If what we know of Alfred and his peers must always be treated circumspectly, examined for where the knowledge originates and how isolated it appears, then much of what we hear in any greater detail of these Vikings has the reliability of a fairy tale. Their movements are reasonably well reported across England and Frankia by different chronicles, but their individual leaders, their motives, how they lived and how they fought are much less thoroughly understood. The leaders of the Great Army that landed in 865, for example, are known in a combination of legend and contemporary record that is impossible to disentangle. The names most strongly associated with the original leadership of the Army are those of three brothers: Ivar ('the Boneless'), Halfdan and Ubba. They are sometimes described as the sons of Ragnar Lothbrok (which means 'of the hairy breeches'), but Ragnar exists almost exclusively in legendary tales. One of those, for which there is not the slightest corroboration, is the thirteenth-century saga that tells of Ragnar being captured by Aella, king of Northumbria, and thrown into a pit of snakes.

The invasion of 865 is thus explained as a filial revenge mission. Unsurprisingly, this story didn't find much currency with English writers of successive centuries, less because it is so unlikely to be true (Aella was not a king at all at the time) than because, as a myth, it served them no useful purpose. Neither lack of evidence nor contradictions within it, as we have already seen with Alfred's story, is an impediment to tales taking hold. Ragnar's story was told by Scandinavian writers of later centuries and, it has been speculated, became particularly important to inhabitants of the English Danelaw, that area of northern England where Scandinavian settlement took permanent hold in the years after Alfred's reign. On this argument Ragnar became part of a founding myth of a society that was destined to be absorbed into its surroundings, explaining why its popularity didn't last as well as that of Anglo-Saxon equivalents.

This myth would have to wait for Hollywood to rediscover it, and reappears in entertainingly garbled form in the Kirk Douglas epic *The Vikings* (1958), where the revenge motif is played out for all it is worth, and Ernest Borgnine, as Ragnar, throws himself into a pit of ravenous wolves, presumably more photogenic than snakes.

THE BLOOD-EAGLE

The leaders of the Great Army, whether Ragnar's sons or not, were of Danish origin, but their activities seem to have ranged across Britain and Ireland, with leaders of the same or similar names popping up in Dublin, Strathclyde and possibly even Frankia. The Anglo-Saxon Chronicle gives little insight into the way these men lived or fought. One abiding legend associated with these brothers, for example, emerges only in much later tales. It is the story of King Aella of Northumbria and the sacrifice of the blood-eagle. The details of this story vary, but they are alike horrifying. According to Sigvtar, a Danish poet of the early eleventh century, Aella was captured at the Battle of York and sacrificed by Ivar to Odin. 'Ivar, who dwelt at York, carved the eagle on Aella's back.' Another version, from the thirteenth century, makes Aella the offering in a more complicatedly awful ritual, in which the living victim has his ribs torn away and his lungs removed and draped over the spread ribs to form the 'wings' of the eagle.

Did the blood-eagle sacrifice really happen? The short answer is we don't know. If we see the Viking invasions in purely political terms, and the Vikings as merely an expansionist people looking for new territory to occupy, as the Anglo-Saxons themselves had been centuries before, then such a lurid tale sounds like the product of an over-vivid imagination. Even though the later accounts in which it is found are Scandinavian, they were written after conversion to Christianity and could have a vested interest in showing their pagan forebears as savagely unenlightened. One historian has called the approach of these writers one of 'antiquarian revival'. Asser and the Chronicle are silent on the subject. Other, more circumstantial, points have been introduced, however, which, while not proving the case either way, might dissuade us from rejecting it out of hand. It has been argued that the late written versions of this story preserve a trustworthy oral tradition (although other details in these sagas, such as the idea that the Viking expedition was a revenge mission by the sons of Ragnar, have been dismissed). It has been pointed out that there was an Old Norse word for 'blood-eagle' (*blothorn*), and it must have referred to an identifiable ritual. A tenth-century Arab visitor to a Viking camp on the Volga described the sacrifice of a slave, so human sacrifice itself was not unknown at this time among pagan Vikings. But the status of kings and slaves was, of course, very different, and the fact that Anglo-Saxons and others were willing to exchange high-ranking hostages with the Vikings as part of the terms of a peace settlement would surely make it unlikely that princes were known to be offered as sacrifices. Equally, as Richard Abels has argued, the co-operation of Archbishop Wulfhere with the Vikings after their victory at York would appear extremely two-faced if they had recently made a pagan sacrifice of the Northumbrian king (though that would not make him the first or last senior churchman to rate survival more highly than Christian principle). The ritual of the blood-eagle is also found in another saga, from the Orkneys, where a king performs the same gruesome actions on a defeated usurper as those described in the most luridly detailed versions of the Aella story.

While the accuracy of the story of the blood-eagle cannot be tested with any degree of certainty, its preservation is instructive in other ways. In particular, it adds to the impression given elsewhere that the Vikings and Anglo-Saxons saw themselves as engaged in a war of religion. And Aella is not the only Anglo-Saxon king whose death takes on the character of a human sacrifice. The details of the death of King Edmund are related by a monk, Abbo of Fleury, eager to promote a Christian version of events. In Abbo's version, written in the tenth century (985–7), Edmund is captured by the Vikings, and, in an echo of the fate of St Sebastian, tied to a tree and shot with arrows. Here again, however, comparisons with Scandinavian rituals as described in the sagas have been made, to argue (as Alfred Smyth has done) that 'Death from piercing ... was the standard form of human sacrifice to Odin.'

Edmund as St Sebastian and Aella as blood-eagle sacrifice, whether legend or history, may be more than religious rationalisations after the events. We are familiar with the workings of medieval Christian piety, the process of martyrdom, the symbolic significance of Christians sacrificing themselves for their faith. But there is no reason to suppose that religion didn't matter to the Vikings too – perhaps as much as it did to the more demonstrably pious Alfred and his family. Portraying the conduct of these wars as instances of 'the cult of Odin' and its assault on Christianity seems neither anachronistic nor far-fetched. In Viking-held areas the institutions of the Church, as well as their material possessions, suffered greatly. Three bishoprics disappear from the historical record about this time, while others would be transferred out of harm's way or find their sphere of activity restricted to those areas still under Christian – that is, eventually only West Saxon – control. True, some Viking leaders were willing to convert to Christianity, but that does not mean that their paganism wasn't sincerely held – merely that they took a practical view of the power of religion to influence their destiny. When victory favoured pagan followers, the Vikings observed their rituals. When it didn't, they could be persuaded, as Anglo-Saxon pagans had been before them, of the power of the Christianity of their victorious enemy.

THE RAVEN BANNER

The story of the capture of the Vikings' Raven Banner takes a more ambivalent view of the religion of the 'enemy', and it brings us closer to Alfred's confrontation with them. It also has more contemporary corroboration than the human sacrifice stories. The Anglo-Saxon Chronicle mentions the capture of the banner in Devon in 878 from a Viking outflanking force led by one of the sons of Ragnar, Ubba. This was at the time that Alfred was hiding out in Athelney, gathering his strength to attempt to retake his kingdom, so it was one of his ealdormen (senior nobles) who won this victory. Apart from a ship, the banner is the only item captured by the Anglo-Saxons to be mentioned in the Chronicle for this time, so its significance cannot be dismissed. The raven was Odin's bird in mythology, and a bird of war in practical terms, since it feeds on carrion. Ravens appear throughout Viking mythology of a later date, for example as interlocutors in a poem celebrating the achievements of the tenth-century king of

Norway, Harald Finehair ('We've been comrades of Harald, Halfdan's son, / ... since we broke from the egg').

Later tales of the Raven Banner would give it magical properties. According to the twelfth-century Annals of St Neots (which also includes a version of the story of Alfred and the cakes), the banner was one of four woven by three daughters of Ragnar Lothbrok, the sisters of the original leaders of the Great Army, in a single hour. The raven embroidered on it could predict victory: if it fluttered, the Vikings would win; if it drooped, they would lose. Like the blood-eagle and the martyrdom of Edmund, the story does not directly involve Alfred, though he is much closer to it, but it would continue to be told for centuries, appearing in popular versions of Alfred's life in ways that skate over what the victorious West Saxons might have thought of the trophy, concentrating on the Vikings' 'losing heart' at forfeiting their lucky charm. As good Christians fighting a war of religion, the West Saxons might have been expected to dismiss the banner as pagan hoodoo, but most versions of the tale seem to take on the Anglo-Saxon Chronicle's attitude of treating something of significance to the enemy as having symbolic significance to the Anglo-Saxons. A comparison can be made with a passage in the Chronicle that tells of Alfred compelling the Vikings to swear an oath on their 'holy ring', 'which they would not do before to any nation'. Alfred's use of the pagans' own ritual objects was sufficiently embarrassing for Asser, when retelling this story, to have the Vikings swear on Alfred's personal collection of holy (Christian) relics. For their part, the Vikings' attitudes to the sanctity of any religious object, their own or their enemies', are probably better indicated by the fact that they broke this oath in 876 (and killed the hostages they had exchanged with Alfred), rather than that they made it. But

8. The capture of the Raven Banner is re-enacted at Winchester, 1901, with Vikings wearing their traditionally inaccurate horned helmets.

the Anglo-Saxon point of view as manifested in the Chronicle seems to have been that the Vikings' paganism was worth taking seriously, even while it was being resisted.

Later versions of the Raven Banner story tend to make a significant, symptomatic change: they put Alfred back into it. For example, at the millenary celebrations at Winchester of Alfred's death, held in 1901 (scholarly redating of Alfred's demise from 901 to 899 happened too late for arrangements to be changed), guests were treated to a re-enactment of the capture of the Raven Banner at the mayoral reception. A photograph exists of this medievalist's Iwo Jima, reproduced in the book that was issued to commemorate the whole event, but it is described in accompanying text as the capture 'at Edington' of the banner: that is, at the great battle later in the same year as the Devon battle (878), when Alfred's forces defeated the Vikings and were at last able to impose terms on them. So by the turn of the nineteenth century the story of the Raven Banner, with its mystical overtones, far from being marginalised, had been pulled even closer to the centre of Alfred's myth.

ALFRED AND GUTHRUM

Alfred had many Viking enemies, but only one has really stuck in the historical imagination: Guthrum. The battles Alfred fought against Guthrum, and Alfred's more or less forced conversion of his defeated enemy after Edington, bring together the personal and religious elements that have been essential to simplifying the messy, multi-layered reality of the Viking wars. Command over the Great Army seems to have passed at some time in the 870s from the sons of Ragnar to Guthrum, who first appears in the Chronicle in 875. It was with Guthrum that Alfred negotiated in 876 at Wareham (where the ineffective oath on the 'holy ring' was sworn and the hostages exchanged and later killed by the Vikings), Guthrum whom he chased the following year to Exeter, with whom he made peace again, and who broke the peace around Twelfth Night 878, when the Viking commander led his army to the royal estate of Chippenham and drove Alfred and his retinue into hiding. It was Guthrum, too, whom Alfred finally defeated at Edington in 878, and who agreed to be baptised and retire to East Anglia, a trusted or at least tolerated Christian king.

In fact, Guthrum emerged as Alfred's chief nemesis only gradually. It is not just that he is not mentioned as a leader of the original Great Army that arrived in 865. Even when he first appears, ten years after that, it is as one of three

9. A coin of Guthrum, bearing a version of his Christian name, Aethelstan.

Viking chiefs, with Oscetel and Anwend, possibly newly arrived from the Continent to try their luck in England. Although these two were apparently part of the initial attack on Wareham, by 878 Guthrum seems to have been in sole command. But even in this crucial year the contest cannot be reduced to the duel of two leaders, because yet another Viking force, the one with the Raven Banner, appeared in Devon, probably led by the last son of Ragnar, Ubba, and defeated there; if that force had been successful, Alfred's contest with Guthrum would have been compounded by another serious threat. The Raven Banner story, moreover, was later connected with Guthrum as unjustifiably as it is connected with Alfred, to give a picture of a straight fight between two leaders. This fight can then be further distilled when Guthrum loses and makes a personal, and in England unprecedented, commitment to convert to Christianity.

The converted Guthrum took the baptismal name Aethelstan, and by the terms of the Treaty of Wedmore, made around 886, was confirmed in his possession of East Anglia.

Coins have been found with Guthrum's new, Christian name on them, demonstrating that he ruled as a king and perhaps also that he took his adoption of Christianity seriously (no coins with his birth name have been found). But almost nothing is recorded about him; almost anything we know about a Viking even as recognisable as Guthrum comes from what Anglo-Saxon accounts say in passing. The fact that the two main contemporary sources, the Chronicle and Asser, were both inspired if not controlled by Alfred himself can allow us to suggest that the king was not interested in affording his opponent a bigger part in his story than absolutely necessary. Asser mentions Guthrum only fleetingly, and even when, in 885, his men are accused of breaking 'in the most insolent manner the peace which they had established with King Alfred', Guthrum is not cited by name. The habit of not naming Alfred's opponent caught on in later centuries. In *Alfred: A Masque*, for example – James Thomson and David Mallet's entertainment for Frederick, Prince of Wales, first performed in the grounds of Cliveden House in 1740 – the 'Danish king' is never named, though he laments the loss of a son, Ivar, thereby suggesting that he is the semi-legendary Ragnar, rather than the more historical Guthrum.

THE VIKINGS REHABILITATED

Thomson and Mallet's Danish king is surprised as he sleeps in his tent, and in other later renditions of Guthrum's story his eventual capitulation, even perhaps his espousal of a gentler religion, is foreshadowed in a portrayal as an effete lover of luxury. In one of the most famous legendary stories of Alfred's reign (to which we will return in Chapter 4), Alfred disguises himself as a minstrel and sneaks into Guthrum's camp on

10. Daniel Maclise's painting Alfred the Saxon King (Disguised as a Minstrel) in the Tent of Guthrum the Dane *(1852): William of Malmesbury's tale filtered through a Pre-Raphaelite lens.*

the eve of the Battle of Edington. William of Malmesbury first told this story in the *Gesta Regum Anglorum*, written in the twelfth century. Alfred, William writes, reported back to his men 'how idle the enemy were and how easy it would be to defeat them'. This picture became part of the standard version of the story, and the portrayal of Guthrum and his men became ever more decadent. In Daniel Maclise's painting of *Alfred the Saxon King (Disguised as a Minstrel) in the Tent of Guthrum the Dane* (1852), for example, the Vikings have become almost orientalised, reclining on cushions as the glowering, red-headed Alfred looks in barely disguised revulsion around him. In the left foreground of the picture the conflation of Vikings and decadent Orientals is made even more explicit, in the figure of a presumably Danish soldier who wears a tunic with an exotic Chinese dragon embroidered on the back, and a Saracen's helmet with spike.

Maclise's attribution of a sort of cultured indolence to the Vikings actually represents an aspect of a rehabilitation of their image that had begun about a century earlier. Maclise's Danes are enfeebled by luxury, but they are emphatically not the savages of earlier portrayals. The popular view of the Viking invaders began to become more favourable only in the second half of the eighteenth century; the visit to England of King Christian VII of Denmark in 1768 has been seen as a contributory factor in this revival. In the same year Thomas Gray's *Norse Odes* were published, and around this time Horace Walpole, dedicated follower of fashion, described himself as 'buried in Runic poetry and Danish wars'. But no similar revival occurred with Guthrum's own reputation. Not only was he always to remain in the shadow of his vanquisher, especially during the nineteenth-century preoccupation with all things Alfredian, but even when the more gruesome aspects of Viking practice were taken up for study (and even for celebration) in the twentieth century it was Ivar the Boneless, son of the legendary Ragnar, initiate of the 'cult of Odin', rather than Guthrum, who became the focus of attention.

In present-day Britain and even in the United States dozens of Viking re-enactment societies gather to re-create the Danish wars. The portrayal of the wars as a clash of religions, beginning with the earliest reports, reinforced by later medieval religious chroniclers and subsequently refined and reapplied to suit the preoccupations of later centuries, has been replaced by a more 'caring' picture for a more sensitive age. The introduction to one British re-enactment society makes the point: 'as the knowledge of historians and archaeologists improves year by year, the image of the Viking Age as a time of abrupt violence is becoming merely a footnote, and the enormous cultural heritage of what is known as the Viking Age is coming to the fore'. That the Vikings may have been capable of great violence as well as the begetters of an 'enormous cultural heritage' is a less popular insight (though one regularly made by historians).

As for Alfred, we began this chapter by saying that the Vikings were the people against whom the king defined himself. In some senses his victory, and his ability to consolidate it by conversion and treaty, enabled the eventual popular rehabilitation of his enemy as less threatening than previously alleged. But that rehabilitation could only begin in a more secular society and has little to do with the real nature of the Vikings' threat or, perhaps more importantly, with how severe the West Saxons perceived that threat to be. As long as paganism remained on the offensive, the Vikings were seen as beyond understanding. In a recent novel about the time of Alfred the Great the hero, an Anglo-Saxon brought up among the Vikings, succinctly describes the alteration in the twenty-first-century view, though it is meant to convince as a ninth-century one: 'to exchange [his Viking protector] Ragnar's freedom for Alfred's earnest piety seemed a miserable fate to me'. As we will see later in this book, Alfred was once a kind of avatar of 'English freedom'. That the opposite view should now be quoted is a good illustration of the kaleidoscopic changes Alfred's achievement and his time have undergone.

3

THE SOLDIER KING

The two best-known statues of Alfred – Count Gleichen's in the king's birthplace, Wantage, from 1877, and Hamo Thornycroft's millennial colossus in Winchester, from 1901 – both depict the warrior at rest. Gleichen, a relative of Queen Victoria and a retired naval officer of some distinction (he had once been recommended for the Victoria Cross), modelled Alfred leaning on a battleaxe, almost as a gardener rests on his spade, his manual work done, his eyes set on nobler things, represented by the scroll he carries in his left hand. Thornycroft's more energetic depiction has Alfred holding his sword aloft by the top of the hilt, perhaps a gesture of victory but also an obvious message of Christian redemption, as the sword held this way becomes a cross. This Alfred's left hand rests on a massive circular shield, and he appears about to take a stride forward, more a man of action than of contemplation. The most recent sculpture of Alfred, by William W. Underhill for Alfred University in New York State (done in 1990: the town itself was named after the king in the nineteenth century), avowedly concentrates on the king as educator, showing him with open book in hand – perhaps that handbook, or 'enchiridion', full of 'pleasing passages' from Alfred's reading to which Asser refers. But it also shows him equipped for war, leaning on his shield in

11. Hamo Thornycroft pictured by the cast of his Winchester statue.

the same manner as Thornycroft's Alfred, his sword scab-barded but in evidence.

Barely a year of Alfred's adult life went by when he wasn't soldiering: if not actively fighting, then preparing defences against the next onslaught. But the statues follow a tradition initiated by and around Alfred himself, in which he is depicted as a warrior-king by necessity, and one with different priorities, such as religion and education. In some ways Alfred's own apparent preference for 'wisdom' over 'warfare' – the words he twinned in the preface to one of his translations as the attributes of a successful king – has distracted us from the plain facts of his life. Alfred was more than just a warrior-king, but he was a soldier before he became king, and he remained a soldier throughout his reign.

On the face of it Alfred's military success, the foundation of everything else he achieved, followed a reasonably simple trajectory. It was one that his own biographer, as well as the Anglo-Saxon Chronicle probably compiled under his influence, set out strongly. At the beginning of his reign, and for seven years, Alfred faced unrelenting attacks, which almost succeeded in driving him out of his own kingdom. By defeating Guthrum's Vikings at Edington in 878 he managed once and for all to make Wessex safe. But the trouble we have with Alfred's decisive victory over Guthrum is that we don't really know how he did it, or what exactly it amounted to. The overall picture of near-failure followed by complete triumph seems to conceal a more complicated situation, but the details are difficult to make out. At times Alfred's position may have been worse than the impression given in the contemporary sources, at times less dire; and even the 'final' victory of Edington may not have been quite as cut and dried as it can be made to appear. In general, the account in the

Chronicle and Asser of the campaigns Alfred fought in this first part of his reign, and then of the one fought at the end against a new Viking enemy, is messy and confusing. The locations of many of the battles are disputed or completely unknown. Numbers, tactics, chains of command are all but impossible to glean reliably from the narrative sources.

The battle narratives are the place where Alfred's world can seem most distant from our own. The cascade of unfamiliar names (Alfred's own name, of course – which means 'Elf-counsel' – would seem as odd to us if it weren't for his having made it famous), the difficulty of imagining what a ninth-century battle consisted of, the doubts over how communications could be relied on over the relatively large distances fought: all these make Alfred's campaigns more difficult to come to terms with than many other facets of his life. We run the risk either of attributing too much control to the participants in what must have been a chaotic business, or of underplaying the seriousness, and possibly the organisation, of the threats Alfred faced.

So Alfred the soldier is important, but it is very difficult to pin down in detail how. Another puzzle about this aspect of Alfred's life is that it also doesn't form a very strong part of his myth. While Asser and the Chronicle give blow-by-blow accounts of the campaigns, it is noticeable that of all the stories and legends that have attached themselves to Alfred's person, very few have to do with him actually fighting. A 1989 book entitled *Alfred the Good Soldier* makes admirable strides in reconstructing the course of Alfred's battles, the ground over which they were fought and the extent of the system of defence that he subsequently put in place, a system that passed a stern examination when a second Viking invasion, fourteen years after Alfred's original enemies had been pacified, arrived in Wessex in 892 (see Chapter 5) But of Alfred's battle tactics, or his personal conduct on the battlefield, not only do we know very little, but very little has even been imagined.

Different pieces of evidence, from archaeology, law codes and charters, can give us something of a sense of the military organisation of Alfred's Wessex. The divisions in society from which his army was drawn can most easily be pictured by comparing the blood money prices set by law on different ranks' heads. Anglo-Saxon law tried to regulate blood feuds by assigning these compensations, called *wergild*, to be paid to a dead man's family by those responsible for his death. A noble, known as a thegn, was worth twice the price of a minor landowner and six times more than an ordinary freeman. The members of an even more exclusive class, the ealdormen, were often of royal blood and are associated with large tracts of land: 'earl' was the Scandinavian equivalent, whose survival shows how successful the Vikings would eventually become in England.

It is from these classes that the king's regular attendants – who often bore witness to his property transactions and are the 'men who serve me' remembered with a gift of £200 in Alfred's will – were drawn. Alfred's 'court', at least until he began to recruit learned churchmen to his household, was probably a rough place populated by men for whom fighting and hunting were the chief occupations. Thegns were a warrior class, armed with swords and embossed shields. For the lower echelons, probably small landholders rather than landless peasants, who could be summoned in a general levy for the defence of their homeland, ash spears were the usual weaponry. The Vikings who faced them were probably armed along the same lines, with swords for the higher ranks and spears for the lower. We read of 'shield-walls' in battle, so we can imagine tightly packed formations pressing against each other, gradually disintegrating as one side gained the upper hand. It was a type of warfare that relied on numbers and morale more than tactics, and it would continue largely unchanged up to the Norman Conquest. The changes that did come were more to do with defensive organisation than innovations on the open battlefield.

BROTHERS IN ARMS

Alfred's military experiences began at his brother Aethelred's side, when the latter was king. In the year 868 the Viking forces that had arrived three years earlier, invading Northumbria after having been (temporarily) bought off in East Anglia, turned their attentions to Mercia, the neighbouring kingdom to the north of Alfred's Wessex. Its king, Burgred, was Alfred and Aethelred's brother-in-law, married to their sister Aethelswith. When the Vikings occupied the town of Nottingham, Burgred requested ('humbly', Asser says) the West Saxons' help. So Alfred's first encounter with his constant enemies was as an ally of the Mercians. It must have been a frustrating experience. The brothers

> gathered an immense army from every part of the kingdom, went to Mercia and arrived at Nottingham, single-mindedly seeking battle. But since the Vikings, protected by the defences of their stronghold, refused to give battle, and since the Christians were unable to breach the wall, peace was established between the Mercians and the Vikings, and the two brothers, Aethelred and Alfred, returned home with their forces.

It was better than a defeat, but the peace Asser mentioned is bound to have come at a price. The 'Danegeld' is popularly associated with Anglo-Scandinavian wars of more than a century later, but if the name had not yet been coined, the principle was still the one Kipling described in his famous poem: 'It is always a temptation to an armed and agile nation / To call upon a neighbour and to say: – "We invaded you last night – we are quite prepared to fight, / Unless you pay us cash to go away".' That was the reality of 'making peace', the phrase that crops up so often in Asser and the Chronicle in this period. Perhaps the West Saxons, as allies rather than the principal adversaries, would not have been expected to contribute to whatever sum of money was demanded by the Vikings to agree to leave Mercia. But the expense of raising and transporting an army, even if not 'immense', would have made this aborted expedition more than exasperating. We can assume that, as well as depleting West Saxon resources, however briefly, this episode would have dented their morale. Even in alliance with another kingdom they were powerless to dictate terms to the Vikings or inflict defeat on them. Good relations with the Mercians were obviously thought worth cementing, however, as it was on this expedition that Alfred married a Mercian ealdorman's daughter, Ealhswith.

When the time came to face the Vikings alone, despite occasional successes, things got a lot worse. In 871, three years after the Nottingham débâcle, the Vikings invaded Wessex. They had re-established themselves in Northumbria, and a year earlier had invaded East Anglia, whose king, Edmund, was killed. In Wessex the Vikings adopted the same tactics they had at Nottingham, making swiftly for a stronghold, in this case the 'royal estate called Reading', where they 'constructed a rampart'. This was the beginning of a year in which, according to varying accounts, the West Saxons engaged their enemy in battle six, eight or nine times. And before the end of April that year King Aethelred had died. Alfred, the last of the five sons of King Aethelwulf, assumed the throne ahead of Aethelred's son, who must have been too young at a time of such crisis.

From Reading the Vikings suffered a set-back at first, when a raiding party was confronted by a West Saxon ealdorman, Aethelwulf, at Englefield. Battle was joined, and the West Saxons inflicted a defeat, with, Asser writes, 'one of the Viking earls ... killed and a great part of the army over-thrown'. But the success was short-lived for Aethelred and Alfred. 'Four days after things had happened there' the main body of the West Saxon Army assaulted the well-defended Vikings at Reading. It doesn't sound as if much guile was involved. The West Saxons 'reached the gate of the stronghold by hacking and cutting down all the Vikings whom they had found outside', but the majority of the invaders were clearly awaiting their opportunity. 'Like wolves they burst out of the gate and joined battle with all their might.' The delayed attack was crucial; the 'Christians eventually turned their backs and the Vikings won the victory and were masters of the battlefield'. Worse, the only success story on the West Saxon side, the ealdorman Aethelwulf, was killed.

It is difficult to tell whether the West Saxons learned any military lessons from this defeat, as their victory in the Battle of Ashdown, which came only four days later, is ascribed by Asser to good fortune and 'faith'. But it is possible that Aethelred and Alfred had drawn two conclusions. First, don't attack the Vikings when they are comfortably ensconced in a stronghold. And second, though this is far more speculative, maybe they realised that a delayed assault, as the Vikings had effected at Reading, could be crucial to turning the tide. The Vikings perhaps made a two-part battle plan easier by splitting their forces in half. It is one of the few occasions when Asser, following the Chronicle, gives any indication of the leadership of the force the West Saxons were facing. He explains the Vikings' decision to split into two divisions by alluding to the fact that 'they then had two kings and a large number of earls'. Oddly, the division appears to have been made to keep the kings together in one formation and the earls together in another. One of those kings, Bagsecg, would die at Ashdown. The other is mentioned by the Chronicle, but not Asser, as Halfdan – one of the three sons of Ragnar – who appears to have taken partial control of the army after East Anglia, where his two brothers Ivar and Ubba are mentioned as the leaders.

The division into two parts played into the West Saxons' hands, whether by divine accident or mortal design. They too split their forces in half, and Alfred engaged the enemy first – not, according to Asser, for any tactical reason but because 'Aethelred, his brother, was still in his tent at prayer, hearing Mass and declaring firmly that he would not leave that place alive before the priest had finished Mass, and that he would not forsake divine service for that of men; and he did what he said'. So, like the Vikings at Reading, Aethelred delayed his intervention in the battle, though to read Asser it would appear that all the fighting was done by Alfred, 'acting courageously, like a wild boar'. The Chronicle makes no mention of the delay in Aethelred's joining the battle, just saying that the two brothers fought the two separate divisions of the Viking army. But taken together, Asser and the Chronicle appear to indicate that Aethelred's late arrival turned the tide. As well as King Bagsecg, five earls are named in the casualty list on the Viking side, and 'many thousands' of men.

It certainly sounds like a comprehensive defeat for the Vikings. In 1738 the antiquarian Francis Wise even suggested that the famous White Horse chalk figure at Uffington was carved on Alfred's orders to celebrate it (ignoring the fact that he wasn't actually king at the time). Recent archaeological investigation has suggested that the Horse predates Alfred's period by about 1,600 years, so G. K. Chesterton's description of its origins at a time 'before the gods who made the gods' may be taken as nearer the mark. This is a rare case of Alfred being connected to something much older than his time, but it illustrates the way in which his legend can suck any related story into its orbit. In any case, there was little time for self-congratulation for Alfred and his brother after Ashdown. Only two weeks later the Vikings were able to engage Aethelred and Alfred again, at Basing, and 'after a long struggle' to become 'masters of the battlefield'. Asser doesn't mention another defeat for the West Saxons, at Meretun (an unknown site), which is described in the Chronicle. But around this time both our near contemporary sources speak of reinforcements arriving for the Vikings, Asser of 'another Viking army [that] came from overseas' and the Chronicle of a 'great summer army'. This was probably the army of which Guthrum, Alfred's future opponent and future godson, was partly in charge.

LAST MAN STANDING

When Alfred next faced the Vikings, at Wilton, he was king. His brother Aethelred had died around Easter. Alfred, according to Asser, 'took over the government of the whole kingdom as soon as his brother had died, with the approval of divine will and according to the unanimous wish of all the inhabitants of the kingdom'. Every part of that statement is open to question, not just the conventional invocation of divine will. If there had been any widespread consultation about the next king, the succession wouldn't have taken place as swiftly as Asser claims. Asser's picture of Wessex as some sort of democracy, albeit one where unanimous votes are received for sole candidates, is equally rhetorical: even the well-known Anglo-Saxon circle of king's close advisers, the witan, was an informal body, whose composition, as indicated by witness lists to royal charters, was not fixed. It is not mentioned by name in the Anglo-Saxon Chronicle until over a century later, although the late tenth-century chronicler Aethelweard describes Alfred's son being 'elected by the magnates'. But in Alfred's own case, if there was any sort of succession process to be decided, it was swift, informal and oligarchical. In fact, the existence of Alfred's will, which mentions two assemblies at which his private inheritance, if not his succession to the throne, was disputed, shows that the transfer of power and property may not have been as smooth as Asser makes out. (Aethelred's sons, while too young when Alfred succeeded, were of age by the time Alfred was considering his own successor and passing over his nephews in favour of his son.) But, as Alfred states in the preamble to that will, Wessex and its people 'were all oppressed by the heathen army'. Whatever the niceties of the inheritance, or the spin of Asser's version of events, military necessity dictated that the royal general had to succeed.

So Alfred fought the last battle of 871 in sole command. Unsurprisingly, the outcome at Wilton was little different from most of the battles that year. Alfred's men were even outnumbered in the field, probably as a consequence of the arrival of the new Viking 'summer' army, and defeat was followed this time by a bought peace. Asser says that the 'Saxons made peace with the Vikings, on condition they would leave them; and this the Vikings did'. We don't know the terms of this peace, but they would not have been very favourable to Alfred. His people had been defeated at least four times, including the last three occasions on which they had faced their enemies. Halfdan and his reinforcements had not been ejected from Reading, and they now apparently outnumbered the forces Alfred could mobilise. While the Vikings didn't seem quite ready for a full-scale occupation of Wessex, they were in no hurry to leave permanently. Alfred probably knew, as Kipling put it, that 'if once you have paid him the Dane-Geld / You never get rid of the Dane', but he had little choice.

If Alfred was under any illusions that he had bought only temporary respite, he needed only to take note of where the Vikings went next. They moved to London, a Mercian city, where the Mercians (who, it should remembered, had already 'made peace' after Nottingham, three years earlier) 'made peace with them' again. Although the Vikings travelled to Northumbria, they extracted a further measure of peace from the Mercians in 873, and the following year they cemented their hold over Mercia once and for all by ejecting their king, Alfred's brother-in-law Burgred, who went with his wife to Rome. A puppet king, Ceolwulf, was appointed in Burgred's place, a similar arrangement to the one set up in Northumbria. Alfred's Wessex had shown more resistance to the Vikings than Burgred's Mercia, but in England making peace with the Vikings merely appeared to postpone the inevitable. And Alfred was alone now, the last independent king in England.

It was three years before the Vikings returned to Wessex in force. In the meantime Alfred had had some success against a Viking raiding party, capturing one of their ships in 875. But three years were clearly not enough to effect any fundamental change to the way Wessex was defended, and when the Vikings occupied Wareham in Dorset, in the heart of the kingdom, Alfred could only 'make a treaty' with the latest invaders. Both Asser and the Chronicle make much, in slightly different ways, of the fact that the Vikings, who were now under the command of Guthrum, Oscetel and Anwend (Halfdan and his men had stayed in the north), were prepared to swear oaths to keep the treaty (see Chapter 2). But the military facts remained constant: when the Vikings decided that it would be in their interest to break their oath and kill their hostages (and, presumably, sacrifice those hostages they had exchanged with Alfred), they did. If Alfred thought he had contained the Vikings at Wareham, they showed him that he hadn't. They gave him the slip and rode to Exeter. Alfred, the Chronicle tells us, 'could not overtake them before their arrival in the fortress, where they could not be come at', but at this point he had his first great slice of luck as king.

While the Vikings' land army was able to elude the West Saxons, a large naval detachment ran into trouble. The Chronicle relates that the 'naval force sailed west along the coast and encountered a great storm at sea; 120 ships were lost there at Swanage'. The Vikings must have been severely depleted – 120 ships means a substantial number of men, perhaps as many as 3,600 – and if, as their break-out from Wareham had suggested, they had intended to occupy Wessex more thoroughly and reduce Alfred to the fate of an Edmund or a Burgred, they now had to postpone their plans.

The terms of the subsequent negotiations are naturally presented by the West Saxon sources as showing Alfred operating from a position of strength. At Exeter the Vikings gave Alfred 'as many' hostages 'as he wished to have – and they swore great oaths and kept a firm peace'. But some historians have seen Alfred's position around this time as far weaker, perhaps analogous to that of Ceolwulf, Burgred's 'tributary king' successor in Mercia. The argument is strengthened by the fact that Alfred and Ceolwulf issued very similar coins from the same London mint, as if both were under Viking control. Against that, though Alfred had not been able to inflict a comprehensive defeat on his enemy, he had not been thoroughly crushed either. And the Vikings in Northumbria and Mercia had installed a new man rather than trusting a defeated incumbent. In 877 the invaders went again to Mercia, where they enforced their terms on its quisling king, but Alfred can have been in no doubt that they would return. Making peace with the Vikings, as the East Angles, Mercians and his own people had learned, was merely a delaying tactic.

GUERRILLA WARFARE

Less than a year later they were back. 'In mid-winter after Twelfth Night' 878 the Vikings descended on Alfred at Chippenham, and although neither Asser nor the Chronicle goes into details, the attack seems to have been completely unexpected. Chippenham was a royal vill, a place where renders of food and money would have been collected, and is likely to have been especially well stocked for the winter.

As with Nottingham, Reading and Wareham, it was a well-chosen place for the Vikings to seize. Alfred fled, unprepared to put up any defence. The enemy 'occupied the land of the West Saxons, and settled there, and drove a great part of the people over the sea, and conquered most of the others', the Chronicle tells us. It was at this point, seven years into his reign, that Alfred reached his lowest ebb, the period that became the focus of so many stories and representations. It lasted five months. During this time Alfred first conducted some form of guerrilla warfare against the occupying forces before gathering his men to meet them in battle. At Athelney in Somerset, according to Asser, Alfred, 'with a few men, made a fortress … and from it with the thegns of Somerset he struck out relentlessly and tirelessly against the Vikings'.

Despite the Chronicle's dire picture, the extent and depth of the Viking occupation are still disputed. That this latest attack was part of a concerted effort to overcome Wessex once and for all, however, is difficult to deny. Asser says that 'very nearly all the inhabitants of that region [i.e., around Chippenham] submitted to their authority'. While this vague reference can be interpreted strongly or weakly, we can at the very least say that this partial investment of the kingdom is likely to have been a starting-point rather than the purpose of the expedition. The impression of a well-planned invasion is strengthened by the arrival of the last of the sons of Ragnar, thought to be Ubba, off the coast of Devon. This was the force that carried the Raven Banner, and by attacking Wessex from the west as well as the east the Vikings surely hoped to cripple the kingdom. Ubba's attack was resisted successfully, at Countisbury. According to Asser, the men of Devon (under the leadership of Ealdorman Odda, a later chronicler tells us) 'overwhelmed their enemy in large part, together with their king, a few escaping by flight to their ships'.

The fact that the men of Devon could raise an army against Ubba demonstrates that neither morale nor military capability had been extinguished by the latest invasion. As for the Vikings, we can't know whether this second invasion formed part of a master plan or just happened to coincide with Guthrum's attack. Towards the end of Alfred's reign, when he faced another great invasion, different Viking armies did seem to work in concert, so it is possible that Ubba's offensive was connected to Guthrum's. If so, it is possible too that the defeat had already put paid to Guthrum's chances of complete success. All these factors complicate the simple picture of Alfred, down and almost out, turning the tables on his exultant enemy.

None the less, Alfred's next move was crucial. If he could gather an army and win, he had a chance. If not, the options would have been to live as an exile or die in battle (the Vikings had not, hitherto, allowed a king who had fought against them to remain even nominally in power). The 'thegns of Somerset', semi-professional warriors who accompanied Alfred on his hit-and-run raids against the enemy, needed to be joined by a more general levy. Later in his reign Alfred would go some way to reorganising the system of military obligation in his kingdom, in particular the way the forti-fied towns, or burhs, were defended. But in 878 he relied on the established loyalties to raise an army. Seven weeks after Easter, in May, Alfred 'rode to Egbert's Stone, which is in the Eastern part of Selwood Forest; and there all the inhabitants of Somerset and Wiltshire and all the inhabitants of Hampshire ... joined up with him'. We can only assume that in the months before this assembly, when Alfred was building his fortress and making his forays from Athelney, he was able to spread the word and appoint a time for those who remained loyal to him in the heart of Wessex to come together.

Asser's description of the king meeting his people again emphasises the extent to which their hopes had been stretched: 'When they saw the king, receiving him (not surprisingly) as if one restored to life after suffering such great tribulations, they were filled with immense joy.' The reinvigorated army struck camp for a night, before moving first to 'Iley Oak' (as with Egbert's Stone and so many of the evocative names in Alfred's campaigns, we don't know where this was), where they spent another night, and then on to Edington, where they encountered Guthrum's army.

Asser and the Chronicle never give a very detailed impression of a battle, but Asser at least tells us that, at Edington, Alfred, 'fighting fiercely with a compact shield-wall against the entire Viking army … persevered resolutely for a long time; at length he gained the victory through God's will'. The West Saxons had, of course, defeated the Vikings before, and this time, as so often, the defeated army was able to flee to some form of safety. With Alfred's men riding after them, they made it back to Chippenham, the royal vill they had occupied so unexpectedly five months earlier and which, one must assume, they had fortified strongly against siege. But, according to Asser, the defeat at Edington and pursuit to Chippenham had left the Vikings less well equipped to cope with a siege. Alfred

> seized everything which he found outside the stronghold – men (whom he killed immediately), horses and cattle – and boldly made camp in front of the gates of

the Viking stronghold with his army. When he had been there for fourteen days the Vikings, thoroughly terrified by hunger, cold and fear, and in the end by despair, sought peace.

As Asser presents them, the terms of that peace were uniquely favourable to Alfred. They were an imposed settlement on a beaten foe:

> the king should take as many chosen hostages as he wanted from them and give none to them; never before, indeed, had they made peace on such terms … When they had been handed over, the Vikings swore in addition that they would leave his kingdom immediately, and Guthrum, their king, promised to accept Christianity and to receive baptism at King Alfred's hand.

It sounds fairly conclusive, and there is no doubt that Guthrum did indeed convert to Christianity, taking the name Aethelstan and ruling and issuing coinage as such in the kingdom that a more detailed peace agreement would establish for him in East Anglia. This is often, and rightly, taken as the most convincing sign that Guthrum had indeed suffered a significant reverse. We should be wary, moreover, of interpreting Guthrum's conversion in purely political terms. Alfred seems to have been a pious man, and it is perfectly believable that Guthrum attributed his enemy's success in part to his faith, just as the pagan Anglo-Saxon kings had been persuaded to Christianity centuries before. We may compare the attitude of the seventh-century Northumbrian king Edwin, who, we are told by Bede, took to heart the argument that 'God has helped you to escape from the hands of the enemies you feared, and it is through His bounty that you have received the kingdom you desired'. So Alfred's magnanimity and Guthrum's good faith may have been all they seemed when, as Asser writes, 'three weeks later ... the King of the Vikings, with thirty of the best men from his army, came to King Alfred at a place called Aller, near Athelney. King Alfred raise him from the holy font of baptism, receiving him as his adoptive son; the unbinding of the chrism on the eighth day took place at a royal estate called Wedmore.'

After Edington, Alfred was definitely able to impose unusually strict peace terms. It may be possible, however, that Edington and its aftermath were no more conclusive a victory than others the West Saxons had had, except for the manner in which they were able to present it. Guthrum's position after the battle cannot have been quite as definitively desperate as Asser makes out. As Asser himself tells us, the Vikings remained in Wessex not just for the few days or weeks that the baptism and treaty ceremonies might be expected to have taken, but for several months. It was not until 879 indeed that Guthrum even vacated Chippenham, and then it was only to decamp to Cirencester, just over the Wessex border, in Mercia, still too threateningly close for comfort. And it was not, in fact, until 880 that the Vikings under Guthrum finally departed for East Anglia; by that time another army, which had arrived the year before, was encamped at Fulham, having 'made contact with the army further upstream' – that is, Guthrum's. Although the Fulham army did leave in 880, apparently without a fight, none of this suggests an Alfred entirely in control of the situation.

So it is possible that the Vikings of Guthrum were not quite the humiliated foe that Asser implies. Perhaps they were just cutting their losses. Halfdan before them had, the Chronicle tells us, 'divided the land of the Northumbrians; so that they became afterwards their harrowers and ploughers' in 876. After so many battles against the West Saxons, and with two serious defeats for their allies at Countisbury and themselves at Edington, Guthrum's men were no nearer to reducing Wessex to the status of the other kingdoms of England than Halfdan and Bagsecg's men had been seven years earlier. We need not doubt the sincerity of his conversion to Christianity to believe that Guthrum had practical reasons too to beat his sword into a ploughshare. And although they settled in East Anglia, and later agreed the division of lands with Alfred by formal treaty, these Vikings were not above joining forces with other raiding parties when it seemed convenient. Not only did they establish contact with the army that set up at Fulham before even having got to East Anglia; but later, in 885, we are told that they broke the truce with Alfred to support another invading army.

We began this chapter with the observation that, despite his success in resisting Guthrum's invaders, no lasting legend has attached itself to Alfred as a warrior in this period. Later, as we shall see, in the second great campaign of his reign, when Alfred had established a system of defence and military organisation that could deal more efficiently with the Vikings, there are stories that stuck, for a time at least. But if we recall that the king must have had great influence over the way these events were related by Asser and the Chronicle, a partial explanation emerges. It was not in Alfred's interests to promote a vision of himself as an invincible warrior whose personal courage would ensure his kingdom's safety. It wouldn't. By allowing Asser and the Chronicle to detail the vicissitudes of the campaigns Alfred could show how difficult it was to inflict any lasting reverse on such a slippery enemy. The difficulty of fighting the Vikings in any conventional fashion was the real lesson of the early campaign. The West Saxons' motto would have to become the scouts': 'be prepared.' Only then would it be understood how necessary were the burdens that the king now imposed on his people to keep up the defence of the realm. Finally, it is difficult to glory too much in the vanquishing of an enemy who subsequently becomes your godson.

Does this attribute too much influence to Alfred over the way his myth was formed? There must be many aspects of the mythical Alfred, from the founder of the jury to the guarantor of regular parliaments, that would come as a surprise to the man himself. But the accounts he would have seen of his military campaigns created the circumstances in which Alfred's prowess as a warrior was underplayed. They also evoked a moment that was ideal for myth-making: the picture of the solitary, unrecognised king on the run in his own land.

4

THE KING OF ATHELNEY: CAKES, SAINTS AND DISGUISES

When Alfred came to translate, as part of his programme of dissemination of 'books which are the most necessary for all men to know', Boethius's *Consolation of Philosophy*, he decided to make a change to the discussion of Ulysses and Circe. Boethius had described the king of Ithaca as resisting the witch's charms, but in Alfred's version Ulysses' love for Circe forfeits the loyalty of his men, who resolve to abandon him as he has abandoned them. It may be inappropriate to impose a twenty-first-century interpretation on this change, detecting the king's 'guilt' at forsaking his own subjects in their hour of need, but Alfred clearly intended something by the variation, and it is not too far-fetched to suppose that he drew on his own experience. For subsequent generations the months when Alfred hid out in Athelney became the distillation of all that was great about the king. At the time of severest hardship he found strength and inspiration. But in Alfred's own time only ultimate victory could have retrospectively justified his actions. Alfred was under no illusions that a king who abandoned his people was a hero.

How, then, did Athelney undergo its transformation from a moment of shame to one of glory? The change can be only partially explained by Alfred's victory at Edington. As we have seen, this triumph may not have been as complete as it was traditionally portrayed. If Alfred's own subjects were to be relied on to defend the kingdom from later attack, they had to be sure that they in turn could rely on their king. So the way the story of his time on the run was told would have been crucial to the re-establishment of Alfred's reputation. In Alfred's own lifetime the Anglo-Saxon Chronicle and Asser began the work of romanticising this period. The Chronicle describes Alfred as he 'journeyed in difficulties through the woods and fen-fastnesses of the moors' with a 'small force' of followers, almost alone among his people in not submitting to Guthrum's army. Asser expands on this a little, writing that 'At the same time Alfred, with his small band of nobles and also with certain soldiers and thegns, was leading a restless life in great distress amid the woody and marshy places of Somerset.' Only after Easter, three months into the Viking occupation, is Alfred described as building a fortress at Athelney, from which 'he struck out relentlessly and tire- lessly against the Vikings'.

Although the near-contemporary accounts give an impression of Alfred's months on Athelney, they leave a convenient vacuum for more imaginative details to fill. What is more, the turnaround in Alfred's fortunes seems so complete after this period that it is tempting to load it with significance. It would not be quite true to say, as Churchill did of El Alamein, that before Athelney, Alfred never had a victory and after it he never had a defeat (it wasn't quite true for Churchill either). But after Athelney, after Edington, and, particularly, after the first draft of their history had been written, it did look as though Alfred was never again in danger of being deposed by a Viking threat. Before, that fate was exactly what was in prospect. More modern historians have speculated that the reforms and programmes of Alfred's later reign may have had their germ in Athelney; but closer to the events themselves Athelney was projected as a place of idyll and miracle, not of policy.

The story of Alfred and the cakes was also one of the oldest of the stories associated with this time, though it was not in Asser or the Chronicle, and not first written down until about a hundred years after Alfred's death. Its high point in popularity came in the Victorian era and the first half, at least, of the twentieth century, well after scholars had shown that there was no contemporary authority for it. Indeed, it is remarkable how often amateur enthusiasts at the turn of the century made pointed remarks about Alfred and the cakes, as a gesture of defiance towards the dry academic stick-in-the-muds who dismissed the story. At the Alfred millenary celebrations in Winchester in 1901, the bishop of Winchester warned that anyone 'so adventurously rash as to discredit on such a day the dear old story of the burnt cakes ... ought not to expect to escape from the doors with a whole skin'. Ten years later, introducing his *Ballad of the White Horse*, G. K. Chesterton wrote of the story: 'It has been disputed by grave historians, who were, I think, a little too grave to be good judges of it.'

In its earliest form, the story is found in a Life of St Neot, probably written in the late tenth century, at least a century after Alfred was actually on Athelney. Neot is a saint whose very existence is open to question, though his tomb is mentioned by Asser. Described as the king's cousin, he is supposed to have predicted to Alfred that he would suffer at the hands of the Vikings and be driven from his kingdom. But if Alfred trusted in St Neot, who would die in the intervening period, the saint's intercession would ensure ultimate victory. If the purpose of the authors of this and subsequent versions of St Neot's life was to make their subject look good (or, at least, real) by attributing to him the triumph of a famous king, then they failed. St Neot's role in the tale of Alfred and the cakes shrank with each successive retelling, as the king's own forbearance took centre-stage.

The Life is written in Latin, and contains some rhetorical flourishes that would disappear in later tellings: the wife who scolds Alfred does so in hexameters, and her oven is described as the 'husband of sea-borne Venus' (i.e., Vulcan, god of fire). In an appendix to Simon Keynes and Michael Lapidge's edition of Asser and other contemporary sources the editors published a translation of this version, as well as three more early adaptations of the tale, the latest of which is dated to the thirteenth century. For all the thousands of retellings over the next ten centuries it is noticeable at first how recognisable the earliest version of the story is. It tells of Alfred, alone and impoverished in his own kingdom, seeking refuge in Athelney in the cottage of an 'unknown swineherd' (in later versions he becomes a 'cowherd', a 'shepherd' and, sometimes in Victorian retellings, a 'neatherd' – which is a cowherd by a quainter name). He was given shelter and stayed for several days, until one day, when the swineherd was out tending his flock, the swineherd's wife put some kneaded flour on the fire to bake. While she busied herself with domestic tasks, the bread burned. The woman rebuked the king ('unknown to her as such'), in the lines of verse that Keynes and Lapidge render as, 'You hesitate to turn the loaves which you see to be burning, / Yet you're quite happy to eat them when they come from the oven'. The king, who had already been pondering the miserable fate that providence had allotted him, did not complain at these harsh words: 'somewhat shaken, and submitting to the woman's scolding, he not only turned the bread but even attended to it as she brought out the loaves when they were ready.'

A HOUSEHOLD TALE

After this earliest recorded telling the story of the 'cakes' (not yet described as such) leads two parallel lives. In the first, the story's natural appeal to ordinary readers and listeners ensured that it was retold countless times over the next thousand years. In this incarnation the story, accepted as a fable, has something of the enduring power of oral tradition. It has been suggested that the written version in the St Neot Life may preserve an older oral tale, thus bringing us closer to the possibility that it began to be told soon after the time it describes. Asser's first modern editor, W. H. Stevenson, commented for example that the story (which in the context of the Life of St Neot is rather plain and unmiraculous), may have originated in a 'tradition connected with Alfred that the author of the Life of St Neot dragged into his compilation when he wearied of filling in gaps of his hero's life from his imagination'. The second strand of life was the one that saw the story being initially accepted by scholars as having contemporary authority, in fact being incorporated as part of Asser's biography of Alfred and then, despite rejection, living on as a notorious instance of legend overtaking fact. Uncovering the background to both these aspects of the story's 'life' is instructive for what it tells us about Alfred and his reputation and about how history is 'constructed' in general.

To take the story's wider appeal first: as one scholar has written, the story's 'point has usually been thought too obvious for any sort of interpretation to be necessary'. But the different embellishments the tale has received over the ages have adapted its popularity to the circumstances in which it was told. Initially, and in essence, it belongs to a familiar genre: the archetype of the unknown ruler bearing tribulation. This genre has an astonishing variety of instances. Alfred himself was certainly familiar with the example of Ulysses, as we have seen, and with biblical instances, such as that of David, the anointed successor to Saul who had to hide from the jealous king, and to some extent that of Jesus himself, when in the wilderness. But the unknown king, adapting to unfamiliarly rude surroundings, recurs throughout literature and history and across cultures. The Hindu avatar Rama is as good an example as Vincentio, the duke of Vienna, who assumes a monk's habit in *Measure for Measure*, or Charles II after the Battle of Worcester.

In fact, perhaps in part because of the influence of the story of Alfred and the cakes, the incognito sovereign crops up surprisingly often in stories of English history, from Richard the Lionheart returning from the crusades to Queen Victoria going among her people (who, unlike the swineherd's wife in Alfred's time, must have had a pretty good idea who she was from the mass reproduction of accurate portraits and likenesses). The point that the ruler must be unrecognised seems to have been subsumed into the idea that there is some intrinsic merit in merely sharing, however briefly, the daily life of the common people. A few years ago the present queen was pictured being served tea in a council flat. There was no suggestion that she was unrecognised, and in some ways her experience was the opposite of the story of Alfred and the cakes: treated politely while she was entertained by a commoner, the queen was widely ridiculed afterwards (mainly for wearing a formal hat). But it may not be completely fanciful to trace the idea that this might have made for good public relations back to the famous tale of her West Saxon forebear.

Throughout the retellings of Alfred's story it is the sign of a virtuous monarch to bear with decorum the indignity of being thought an ordinary citizen. In no version of Alfred's story is he ever imagined saying the equivalent of 'Do you know who I am?' In the first versions of the story Alfred's religious faith is seen to carry him through. He ponders the example of Job or reflects on the same verse in Hebrews that Alcuin quoted to comfort the monks of Lindisfarne after the Viking raids: 'Quem Dominus diligit, castigat; flagellat autem omnem filium quem recipit' – 'He whom the Lord cares for, he chastises; he whips every one of the sons he receives.' The original rendering of the story appeared, of course, in a saint's Life.

In subsequent versions the king's religious devotion is played down, and his practical, martial qualities are emphasised. This alteration begins with the rendition in the twelfth-century so-called 'Annals of St Neots' – in fact, a compilation of mostly East Anglian events – which describes the king 'sitting by the fire … busy preparing a bow and arrows and other instruments of war', and so ignoring the burning bread. The Annals' version was the one to be added into editions of Asser's biography. So it is this Alfred who becomes enshrined in more modern versions, and its more didactic quality, concentrating not on the king's misfortune but on his planning how to respond to it, perhaps explains the transition of the story from pulpit to nursery. In Dickens's *A Child's History of England*, the king, 'being at work on his bow and arrows, with which he hoped to punish the false Danes

12. *Francis Wheatley's* Alfred in the House of the Neat-herd *(1792),*
shows Alfred so engrossed in his archery preparations that he forgets the cakes.

when a brighter time should come, and thinking deeply of
his poor unhappy subjects whom the Danes chased through
the land ... forgot the cakes, and they were burnt'.

Before the printing of Asser's text in the sixteenth century, other details were imported or invented for the story. Several chroniclers, from Florence of Worcester in the twelfth century to the fifteenth-century verse Chronicle of John Hardyng, name the swineherd and his wife, giving the common people as significant a role in the tale as the king. The swineherd, Denewulf, was even said to have been elevated later to the bishopric of Winchester. This aspect of the tale is still going strong in H. E. Marshall's *Our Island Story* (1905), where the author straight-facedly explains that 'Alfred made the swineherd a bishop, for he had found out while hiding in his cottage that Denewulf was a good and wise man'. More generally, the honest, merry English peasant aspect of the story would continue to find favour until at least the seventeenth century, the period of a ballad that puts the swineherd's wife centre-stage. It was the suffering and forbearance of the king, however, that won out until recent years, establishing the tale as exemplary rather than entertaining.

From a modern perspective the serious element to the tale has all but vanished. No longer is the appeal of the story of the cakes, in David Hume's words in the late eighteenth century, that of 'so much dignity reduced to so much distress'. Unsurprisingly in an age that takes its kings less seriously, the story now is more likely to be played for laughs, if at all. Admittedly, the comedy wasn't far away even in early versions, when the thirteenth-century John of Wallingford pictured Alfred taking his chastisement patiently, as always, and then cack-handedly attempting to help 'in the baking operation' despite his 'extremely unskilled hand'. Perhaps it was the substitution of cakes for bread that shifts the tale from the exemplary to the comical (the original Latin circumlocution translates as 'kneaded flour'), but certainly by the time Thackeray wrote in the mid-nineteenth century about a historical painter's super-scale depiction of the famous episode, 'seventy-two feet by forty-eight', in which the 'mere muffin, of which the outcast king is spoiling the baking, is two feet three in diameter', the comics had won. Thackeray even had another go at the vanity of history painters, when the unsuccessful artist Gandish points out his rendition in *The Newcomes*: 'Why is my "Alfred" 'anging up in this 'all? Because there is no patronage for a man who devotes himself to 'igh art.'

Like Robert the Bruce and the spider (which one twentieth-century cartoon neatly conflates with Alfred – 'King Alfred burnt many many cakes. But to his credit, he never gave up'), Alfred and the cakes has ended up a schoolroom joke. For the historian Charles Plummer at the turn of the century, the 'silly story of the cakes' is responsible for a whole misconception of Alfred's greatness. By the time of W. C. Sellar and R. J. Yeatman's *1066 and All That* (1930) he is 'Alfred the Cake', and the lesson that the story isn't historical is filtered in: 'As, however, Alfred could not have been an Incendiary King *and* a good King, we may dismiss the story as absurd.'

When Alfred became the subject of a feature film in 1969, it was decided to leave the cakes out. This decision can hardly be justified in terms of historical fidelity, as the script is in most respects pure fantasy. One can only assume that it was omitted because it was deemed too silly, although scriptwriters who end a film with the line 'Your God of love is very powerful' must have been fairly relaxed about the prospect of unintended comedy. Nevertheless, in the years after the millenary celebrations the bishop of Winchester's 'dear old story' had been wounded less by scholarly sneers than by schoolboy sniggers.

THE EDITOR'S MISTAKE

It was another bishop, in fact an archbishop, Matthew Parker, who at the time of Elizabeth I was responsible for launching the story of the cakes on its parallel voyage of scholarly respectability. Parker, as archbishop of Canterbury, was a semi-official collector of early medieval manuscripts, particularly those, as we saw in Chapter 1, that could be used as evidence of an Early English Church independent of Rome. He had a privy council warrant issued in 1568 to help him procure manuscripts pertaining to the 'conseruation of such auncient recordes and monumentes, written of the state and affaires of these her realms of Englande and Ireland'. This was the work that later got the archbishop associated (probably bogusly) with the nickname 'Nosey Parker', and which eventually produced the lavish *De Antiquitate Britannicae*. He acquired a manuscript of Asser's Life of Alfred some time between 1552, when the previous known owner died, and 1574, when Parker produced the first printed version of the Life. It was this first edition that incorporated the excerpts from the Annals of St Neots, including the story of the cakes.

In an age less scrupulous about techniques of editing, it was an understandable decision. Parker believed that Asser was the author of the Annals (in fact, whoever compiled the Annals had read Asser). St Neot is referred to once in the main text of Asser, when the biographer mentions that a shrine at which Alfred prayed as a young man now contains Neot's grave. It is possible that this reference too is a later interpolation, but it has been equally strongly argued that Asser's remark could provide evidence of a tradition that made the otherwise historically evasive Neot a Cornish hermit who lived around the time of King Alfred. The cakes story itself is not out of keeping with the tone of much that is in genuine Asser, from the intimate details of the king's illnesses and his passions for learning and innovation to the fairly marginal insertion of a lengthy anecdote to explain the West Saxon habit of not granting their kings' consorts the title of queen (where the wicked queen Eadburh ends up, like Alfred, down on her luck, though her situation is permanent: she 'shamefully spent her life in poverty and misery until her death'). Some scholars have even argued that the fact that the cakes story seemed to fit so well into Asser was because the whole book was a forgery, cobbled together from various sources to give a wholly false picture of Alfred (see Chapter 7). But the general consensus remains that Asser really was writing in 893, and the Annals were compiled more than two centuries later.

For all its charm, the story shouldn't have been there, and for almost 300 years, from Parker's edition of 1574 to Henry Petrie's in 1848 (which included the story, but in square brackets to demonstrate it wasn't in the original manuscript), the cakes were passed off as Asser's tale and therefore given the stamp of contemporary authority. The destruction by fire in 1731 of the original manuscript, which had passed into the hands of the collector Robert Cotton, was the final reason for the delay in setting the record straight. Without an original to check against, it was only scholarly detective work that could definitively establish that the story was an interpolation. So by the time of the Alfred millenary at Winchester it was only just over fifty years since the first authoritative dismissal of the story had been published; even the edition of Asser by W. H. Stevenson, printed in 1904, that scholars still use today, contained the story, though in different, smaller type to mark it out. And in his notes Stevenson struck the now familiar tone of the exasperated scholar: 'More mischief has been wrought by Parker's interpolation of this long passage than by any of his other falsifications of historic evidence.'

The initial reason for an early scholar such as Parker to include the story, apart from general plausibility, may be said to have something to do with his wider project of mining the earliest origins of the English Church. The cakes story, with its connection to an English saint, established the piety and purity of Anglo-Saxon Christianity. The fact that Alfred and his line were almost fanatically devoted to Rome, raising alms to send there whenever possible, and making sure the king's childhood audience with the pope was not forgotten, only made it more important to establish an Alfredian link with native piety. So in a sense the cakes story's journey of scholarly credibility is connected to the general trend of Alfred being seen as the quintessential founding father. If Alfred can be linked with something, in later eyes that gives it a stamp of approval. The cakes may have ended up a 'silly story', reduced to the margins of history, but the reasons for its initial acceptance can be seen to be quite central to serious English perceptions of their identity.

The rejection of the story became a badge of professional pride, but it is arguable that rejection produced an even less convincing picture of the king. When Plummer dismissed it, it was because such tales 'besmirch the fair form of our hero king, in order to exalt a phantom saint'. Later historians may be more reticent about using a term such as 'hero king', but there has been no doubt about the continued damage done by the story to the 'true' picture of the king and his experiences. For R. H. C. Davis, in 1971, the cakes were still 'subconsciously influenc[ing] the historical imagination more powerfully than is sometimes realised'. Davis argued that in fact Alfred had not been in so much danger after all in 878. He had allowed the Anglo-Saxon Chronicle and Asser to portray his Athelney experience in fairly desperate terms as a device to ensure that his people accepted 'new and burdensome institutions'. As later readers, we cannot help but add the cakes story to that portrayal to complete the picture of the king in critical circumstances.

Here, dismissing the cakes involves dispensing with everything it represents, as if a lie must be behind a tradition, rather than the equally likely possibility that a colourful story originates and persists because it illustrates, rather than contradicts, the true picture. To say that the cakes story rings true is very different from saying it *is* true. As for the question of whether Alfred himself is really responsible, because of his 'propaganda' methods of exaggerating his experiences in 878: Alfred would have been the last king in England, not the first, to lose his throne to the Vikings. Perhaps Guthrum was not in such a dominant position as he seemed after occupying Chippenham. But we need not be surprised, or suspicious, if Alfred believed he was.

THE MINSTREL AND THE MIRACLE

The story of the cakes was, of course, only the best-known of those that took the time in Athelney as their setting. Another almost as celebrated describes Alfred's stealing into Guthrum's camp before the Battle of Edington. This story

13. A portrayal for children of Alfred in the Danish camp before the Battle of Edington. The author, R. J. Unstead, uses the tale to make Alfred seem approachable: 'the Northmen loved music and they welcomed this merry fellow who sang so well to his harp'.

was first told by William of Malmesbury in the *Gesta Regum Anglorum*, completed around 1125. Alfred

> hazarded a most cunning trick. Dressed as a minstrel he entered the Danish king's camp, supported by one most faithful companion who knew the secret. There, gaining entry as a professional entertainer, even to the innermost quarters, there was no secret that he did not learn with both eyes and ears. After spending several days there and finding out to his heart's content all that he wanted to know, he returned to Athelney, collected his chief men together, and explained how idle the enemy were and how easy it would be to defeat them.

This story, while always remaining more obviously doubtful because of its late origin, became an established part of Alfred's legend, the subject of historians for children as well as adults, and the inspiration for such exuberant artistic treatment as Daniel Maclise's (see Chapter 2). It is also an example of the way that good stories stick to Alfred, for William tells a very similar tale later in his history. In the reign of Aethelstan, Alfred's grandson, a young Viking enemy, Anlaf, is said by William to have employed the same trick of sneaking into the opposition's camp dressed as an 'entertainer'. Here the story is used to demonstrate Viking treachery rather than Anglo-Saxon intelligence. But what is more interesting for our purposes is the fact that this second story is almost completely forgotten.

The last Athelney story, which William also tells, is one, like the cakes, with its source in the life of a saint. This time St Cuthbert appears to the king in a dream on Athelney, promising that 'you shall in a short time be restored in glory to your throne', and as a 'token' of the truth of the prophecy, the saint predicts that Alfred's men will return from fishing with a 'great catch of big fish in their creels', despite the fact that the river is frozen over. 'With these words the saint relieved the sleeping king of all his cares', and Alfred awakes to a 'a huge catch of fish as might seem enough to glut any great army'. Another variation of the St Cuthbert story has him appearing to Alfred as a pilgrim, and the king sharing his last loaf with him. This too became a popular subject for eighteenth- and nineteenth-century history painters, such as Benjamin West (George Washington had a print of the subject at Mount Vernon). Unlike the cakes and the minstrel's disguise story, however, the Alfred and Cuthbert stories have faded from view. We can account for the cakes' popularity in

part because of the accident of Parker's editing which combined it with Asser, but with the relative fortunes of William
of Malmesbury's stories we can compare the appeal of two
tales and how they fit into subsequent portrayals of the king.
The Cuthbert story, with its miraculous element, is a picture
of Alfred for the Middle Ages, an anxious monarch finding
relief in the promises of a saint. The story of the disguise
and the enemy camp, with no explicit religious underpin-
ning, can be imagined by later ages that saw God intervening less directly in mortal affairs. Moreover, it seems to link
back to other aspects of Alfred's character, to his interest in
reading and committing things to memory, even to the book
of 'Saxon poetry' of Asser's childhood tale.

FROM ATHELNEY TO BRITANNIA

So far we have looked at individual stories connected
with this time in Alfred's life, from the most famous to the
most obscure. But in later times it was more the setting of
Athelney itself, combined with the idea of a king without a
real kingdom to rule over, that became the source of inspiration. Alfred clearly remembered Athelney's central place in
the revival of his fortunes, as indicated not only by the way
in which the Chronicle and Asser discuss it, under his influence, but also by the fact that he founded an abbey there.
That foundation lasted until the dissolution of the monasteries by Henry VIII in 1539, and a recent discovery of a
book of medieval charters confirms that the medieval monks
of the abbey around the eleventh or twelfth century were
concerned enough about maintaining their links with their
founder-king to fabricate a charter purporting to originate
from his time. Though no trace of Athelney Abbey remains

14. *The Athelney Monument, a modest memorial raised in 1801 by John Slade, the owner of the farmland, marking the spot where Alfred founded an abbey to commemorate the scene of his lowest fortunes.*

above ground, it is commemorated by a monument raised in 1801.

It was in the eighteenth century that the idea of Athelney as representative of all that was best about England, as a sort of kingdom in miniature, uncorrupted by metropolitan influence, emerged. In James Thomson and David Mallet's *Alfred: A Masque*, expanded by Mallet, after its first private performance, for the London stage (from which text the quotations that follow are taken), this view is much in evidence. The piece may now be remembered only for the intimations of imperial naval supremacy with which it ends, 'Rule Britannia', but the setting is Athelney, an 'isle' whose natural virtues Corin, an unusually prolix shepherd, expounds early on:

> Thou hast not weigh'd
> This island's force; the deep defence of woods,
> Nature's own hand hath planted strong around;

The rough encumbrance of perplexing thorns,
Of intertwining brakes that rise between,
And choak up every inlet from abroad.
Yet more; thou know'st beyond this woody verge
Two rivers broad and rapid hem us in;
Along whose border spreads the gulphy pool,
And trembling quagmire to betray the foot
Its treacherous greensward tempts one path alone
Winds to this plain, so difficult and so strait,
My single arm, against a band of foes,
Could long, perhaps, defend it.

Later this same character, obviously the shepherd of the cakes story transmuted into an ideal of the noble peasant, predicts that 'My humble cottage / Long ages hence, when we are dust, my friends, / In holy pilgrimage oft visited / Will draw true *English* knees to worship there, / As at the shrine of some propitious saint'. If the usual convention of predictions coming true in works written centuries after the events they describe is ignored here, it may be a deliberate admonition to the audience. Athelney *should* be a place of pilgrimage, if only political life weren't so corrupted. And of course, it is English knees that are to be drawn there; any idea of Alfred as a West Saxon king is long gone.

The character of Alfred himself reinforces the sacred view of Athelney: 'this island spot, / Fair freedom's last retreat. We must, we will / Preserve it all inviolate and holy'. The cakes story as such does not appear in the masque, which invents its own incidents, including the capture of Alfred's wife by the Danes, and rewrites history comprehensively. But the way in which Athelney can be used for so specific a purpose as a commentary on eighteenth-century politics demonstrates the pliability of Alfred's myth. The cakes remain the universal story of Alfred partly because of their association with the atmosphere of Athelney, of the king with the opportunity to start from scratch, inspired by the innocence of the heart of his kingdom.

It may be thought that with the legend of Athelney and the various later stories of Alfred's time there, however distant their origins, we are moving very far from the 'historical' Alfred. But it was Alfred, through Asser and the Chronicle, who planted the seed of the Athelney myth. Later historians have argued over the truth of the picture of destitution and abandonment that begins with the Chronicle and Asser's depiction of Athelney and is only elaborated by the following centuries' stories. They see the cakes and other stories as distractions from the possibility of seeing a true picture of the king's activities at this time. But the truth is that Alfred has already made sure that is impossible. We have only his, or his circle's, word for it. Later, in a letter accompanying his translation of Gregory the Great's *Pastoral Care*, Alfred would invoke the time when 'everything was ransacked and burned' as a shared memory. The later stories constructed a myth around it that is in keeping with the outline already drawn in the ninth century. Perhaps, after all, Alfred's adaptation of the story of Ulysses and Circe is as good an indication as any of what happened between Twelfth Night and mid-May 878. The king abandoned his people but returned from Athelney to triumph. What he did while he was there, we can never be sure.

5

DEFENDER AND PARDONER: ALFRED'S ADMINISTRATION AND ITS TEST IN THE LAST CAMPAIGN

The writers of the film *Alfred the Great* (1969) chose to end their screenplay on the field of Edington, after an imaginative battle scene in which the West Saxons are shown performing a series of manoeuvres that combine elements of Trooping the Colour and a Broadway chorus line. A text flutters on to the screen, telling us that 'Here England was united and Alfred was its only sovereign to be called the Great'. We will come in a later chapter to the well-known fact that Alfred did no such thing as 'unite' England. It is the decision to end at Edington that is as interesting, with Alfred still to rule twenty-one more years. The more populist the portrayal of Alfred, it seems, the less space is given to what happened after Edington. The film is merely an extreme example of a tendency to leave the rest of Alfred's reign to the professionals, as if only academic historians could untangle the achievements of the king's later years.

It was not always like that. If the high point of Alfred's popularity was in the nineteenth century, then it is noticeable in the portrayals of Alfred made then how much attention is paid to the king after Athelney, the cakes and Edington.

To many modern historians the greatest of Alfred's achievements was his creation, if not from scratch then from fairly rudimentary beginnings, of a well-administered system of defence to keep his kingdom safe from Viking attack. Some Victorian artists took up an episode when that system was put to the test, during the last great campaign of his kingship, in the story of 'Alfred and Hastings'. The king is depicted allowing the family of a later Viking enemy, 'Hastings', to depart – in one version (by Henry Pierce Bone, 1814), the title being elaborated to explain that the king is 'observing that he did not fight against women and children'.

The story of Alfred and Hastings, whom later historians know better as Hastein, has faded from popular view, though its origins are impeccable. Hastein was an enemy in some ways as formidable as Guthrum had been, and it is clear from the moment that the painters selected that Alfred attempted a similar diplomatic strategy to deal with him as had seemed to succeed with Guthrum. For, as the Anglo-Saxon Chronicle entry for 893 relates, the reason that Alfred was letting the Viking's wife and sons go was not simple clemency, or the chivalric impulse suggested by his supposed reluctance to 'fight against women and children'. It was because one boy was Alfred's godson, and the other was the godson of his son-in-law the Mercian ealdorman Aethelred. The Chronicle explains that 'They had stood sponsor to them before Hastein came to Benfleet, and he had given the king oaths and hostages, and the king had also made him generous gifts of money, and so he did also when he gave back the boy and the woman.'

In fact, Hastein's force was only the smaller part of a two-pronged Viking attack that began in 892 and was not entirely expended until 896. In the years running up to this invasion the Chronicle gives an unusually detailed picture of Viking movements on the Continent, where first the Bretons and then a combined force of East Franks, Bavarians and Saxons defeated a large band. By 892 this beaten 'great army' was ready to try its luck elsewhere. It proceeded to Boulogne, was 'provided with ships' – probably by the local inhabitants, who would have been happy to see the back of it – and sailed over to Kent in 250 vessels. The commander of this great expedition is not named, but 'shortly afterwards' Hastein launched a second attack, up the Thames, with a further eighty ships. Hastein's previous career had ranged across Europe: he was, according to legend, the leader of a raid aimed at Rome almost thirty years earlier. The story goes that the Vikings were so impressed on that occasion with the buildings of Luni, more than 180 miles away, that they sacked the town in the belief that it was Rome. Even if Hastein's activities were less extensive than this story suggests, he was clearly an experienced soldier and an enemy formidable enough to be named by the Chronicle, despite being at the head of a fleet less than a third of the size of the one that had already arrived in Kent from Boulogne. He was also taken seriously enough by Alfred for the king to have attempted to neutralise him (and pay him off) with baptism and gift-giving.

Perhaps another reason that the episode of Alfred and Hastein's family hasn't left an indelible mark on posterity is that the strategy had not worked. In the case of Guthrum, Alfred was operating from a position of strength, even if it was not as impregnable as later commentators may have led us to believe. But with Hastein the sponsorship of his family seems to have been an ineffective opening gambit; the Viking chief had manifestly not kept the peace, and it is as easy to ascribe Alfred's willingness to release his godchildren-hostages 'with generous gifts of money' to an attempt to buy time or buy off his foe as to Christian mercy. But what the course of the war against the two enemies illustrates is that Alfred had also adopted new strategies to defend his realm, strengthening the fortifications of his kingdom and reorganising his army. And in his son Edward the Elder he seems to have found a reliable additional commander. A parallel rarely remarked on between Alfred's resistance of Guthrum and his ejection of Hastein and his ally is that the king's success depended in part on the victory of a second general: in 878, it was ealdorman Odda and his Devonians defeating Ubba's secondary attack at Countisbury; in 893 Alfred's son took on one army, defeating it at Farnham in Surrey while his father guarded Wessex, preparing to relieve him when the time came. In fact, during the course of the war, several significant actions took place when the king himself was otherwise engaged. At Chichester, Exeter, Buttington and on the River Lea 20 miles from London various forces took on the invaders with varying degrees of success. The Anglo-Saxon Chronicle, which gives an extremely detailed account of the course of this war, records much of this but plays down Edward's part, concentrating on Alfred. A version of the events of 893–6 translated into Latin by an ealdorman, Aethelweard, in Edward's own reign, is the only one that allows us to see the son playing a significant role in the father's eventual triumph.

'AN ACRE'S BREADTH OF WALL'

It is to Edward's reign, too, that we must turn for the most compelling evidence of Alfred's defensive reorganisation of Wessex, which was severely tried (and, it should be observed, sometimes found wanting) by the late invasion. This document, dated to around 911–14, is known as the Burghal Hidage. The odd name – which is meant to describe the connection between the fortifications, or burhs, that Alfred built or reinforced, and the land holdings, divided into 'hides' (an area around 40 acres, or one man's holding), on which service in the burhs was calculated – was given by the legal historian F. W. Maitland only at the end of the nineteenth century, and it was in the twentieth century that its significance for Alfred's reign was asserted in a series of articles and studies. The patient teasing out of meaning from a formal administrative account, while the dramatic, illustrative anecdote such as Alfred and Hastein's family is relatively neglected, may be seen as emblematic of the progress of Anglo-Saxon historiography, in which analysis, and an almost private language, has taken over from narrative. The unintentional effect is that less of Alfred remains in popular view. You can't tell a memorable story or paint a picture inspired by the Anglo-Saxon equivalent of a military census.

In its way, however, the Burghal Hidage is every bit as remarkable as Alfred's Christian generosity to Hastein's family, and in some ways far more so (it certainly describes a more effective strategy). It lists, depending on the manuscript consulted, between thirty and thirty-three burhs and gives the assessment of the number of men required to defend and repair them. The evidence of Asser and the Chronicle shows that this system of defences had been established by Alfred, though burhs themselves seem to have been a long-standing Anglo-Saxon method of organisation. It has also been suggested that Alfred may have looked across to Frankia to the defensive measures of his step-grandfather Charles the Bald for dealing with the Vikings. There is an indication in Asser and the Chronicle that Alfred's strengthening of some burhs and creation of others had been put to the test before 892, when a Viking army attacked Rochester in 885. Asser, embellishing the Chronicle, writes that 'The Vikings immediately constructed a strong fortress for themselves in front of [Rochester's] entrance, but they were unable to capture the city because the citizens defended themselves courageously until King Alfred arrived, bringing them relief with a large army'. Kent is not included in the Burghal Hidage, so its assessment of Rochester's needs cannot be checked, but there is certainly a difference between the townspeople's ability to resist this attack and the unpreparedness of a place such as Wareham earlier in Alfred's reign (see Chapter 3).

Wareham is included in the assessment, where it is assigned 1,600 hides (i.e., 1,600 men). The Hidage explains that 'For the maintenance and defence of an acre's breadth of wall, sixteen hides are required', and then goes into more detail of how length of wall corresponds to number of men, allowing us to check the figures with reasonable certainty. The standard of accuracy varies for different places. At Wareham 1,600 men were expected to defend 100 'acre's breadths' (2,200 yards) of wall. It is still possible to walk around the ramparts of Wareham, which were actually re-fortified in the Second World War (demonstrating, at the very least, that Alfred's strategic judgement would survive the test of time). Three sides of the town are bounded by earthworks, and the measurement given in the Hidage corresponds very precisely to these. Some historians, keen to stress the accuracy of the Hidage, have made little of the fact that the measurement doesn't add up if the fourth side of Wareham, which overlooks the River Frome, is included. Vikings, of course, often attacked upriver, and it is inconceivable that this side would have been undefended.

A closer match between the Hidage's assessment and the length of wall is to be found at Winchester, an example described by one historian as 'justly famous'. It is assigned 2,400 hides, which means that 2,400 men were required to defend 3,300 yards of wall, corresponding almost exactly to the Roman walls of the city (measurable now at 3,318 yards), which were already at least 500 years old by Alfred's time. The remarkable match at Winchester has led many historians to see the Burghal Hidage as evidence of an astonishingly well-tuned administrative system in Edward the Elder's time (and by implication also Alfred's, because many of the burhs listed predate Edward's reign and are mentioned in Asser and/or the Chronicle). There has been some dispute of the claim that 'all but two of the Burghal Hidage fortifications come within a 5 per cent margin of accuracy', and it should certainly be admitted that it is tempting to force the figures to match. The more accurate they are, the more remarkable a document the Hidage is and, by implication, the more impressive is Alfred's administrative achievement: another instance where Alfred's 'greatness' prejudges his accomplishments. But the ambition alone indicates a system of government committed to controlling and assessing its resources of manpower in an unprecedented way.

Almost as impressive as the close match in some cases of listed burhs is the total number of men required to work the system, which amounts to 27,071. The great historian of the crusades Sir Steven Runciman once wrote that 'Every medieval historian, whatever his race, invariably indulges in wild and picturesque exaggeration whenever he has to estimate numbers that cannot easily be counted', but here, for a much earlier period, we have a credible, verifiable count of the sort of numbers expected to assist in the defence of a realm. Population estimates are notoriously inaccurate for this period, but most figures hover around the half a million mark for Wessex, which means that around 5–6 per cent of the population was engaged in burghal defence. And, of course, Alfred also had to summon armies into the field, which sometimes had to operate over great distances. When, in his version of Boethius's *Consolation of Philosophy*, Alfred is the first recorded writer to refer to the subsequently widespread notion of a society divided into 'praying men, fighting men and working men', he is clearly thinking of a rather larger proportion of the second group than a modern reader is used to.

The debate over Viking numbers has tipped in recent years towards trusting the contemporary sources more. But even the maximalist view of the enemy's strength means that they were vastly outnumbered by the budgeted manpower of Wessex. Alfred seems to have been determined that never again, as in the first year of his reign at Wilton, would his troops be 'easily outnumbered'. It was only by the organised marshalling of superior numbers that the defenders could hope to counteract the attackers' freedom and manoeuvrability. If the Vikings could strike at will, the West Saxons had to be prepared to defend wherever the fancy had taken them.

THE LAST WAR

To this end, it seems that Alfred not only set up an integrated system of fortifications but also reformed the way the army served. In its account of the invasion of Hastein and Co., the Anglo-Saxon Chronicle explains the changes Alfred had made. 'The king', we are told in the entry for the year 893, 'had divided his army into two, so that always half its men were at home, half on service, apart from the men who guarded the burhs.' It is extremely difficult to make out exactly how this division worked in practice. Asser doesn't refer to this particular division of West Saxon resources, but in Chapters 99–102 of the Life he shows the king to have a penchant, one might almost say a mania, for division. Asser's Alfred divides his time, his household, his money, his revenue and his donations. The household, according to Asser, was divided into three parts, with a one-month-on, two-months-off division of labour. Unfortunately, this does not seem to correspond to the military division (and would in any case make for a very disjointed campaign if personnel were being swapped every month). The Chronicle tells us that one division of the West Saxon army, which was besieging a force of Vikings at an island in Buckinghamshire in 893 (and which must have been the force commanded by Alfred's son), stayed,

> for as long as their provisions lasted; but they had completed their turn of service and used up their provisions, and the king was then on his way there with the division which was serving with him. When he was on his way there and the other English army was on its way home … the Danes were remaining behind there because their king had been wounded in battle.

This gives no clear picture of how the terms of service worked. One innovation seems to have been that the army had its own provisions, so that it was not required to live off the land (which the Vikings would often have denuded of supplies). But in this case provisions ran out before relief had arrived, and, considering the Chronicle states that they stayed 'as long as their provisions lasted', it is possible that this army actually exceeded its term of service in order to wait for relief and only turned for home because it could hold out no longer, rather than because its time was up.

In fact, the whole account of the war of 892–6 in the Chronicle, though unusually full, is so confusing that very few wider conclusions can be safely drawn from it. As we have seen, it is only a later chronicle by Aethelweard, a late tenth-century West Saxon nobleman, that names the commander of the army that defeated the Viking force at Farnham as Alfred's son Edward. The focus of the Anglo-Saxon Chronicle on Alfred is so restricting that it doesn't even give this information. The story it tells is of a combined invasion lasting over three years, beginning in 892 and not departing Wessex until the summer of 896.

The invaders began in Kent, the two Viking armies building fortresses for themselves at Milton and Appledore, about 20 miles apart. The following year, the Chronicle alleges that the settled Danes of East Anglia and Northumbria (the remnants of the armies of the 860s and 870s) joined the new invaders, 'contrary to [their] pledges', and 'as often as the other Danish armies went out in full force, they went either with them or on their behalf'. It is only in this context that the Chronicle actually has Alfred beginning his confrontation with them, 'twelve months after the Danes had built the fortress in the eastern kingdom' (i.e., Kent). The old pattern of the West Saxons' trying to tempt the well-positioned invaders into battle was resumed. This time Alfred placed himself between the two armies, possibly at Maidstone, and waited for a full break-out from either. The Chronicle seems to contradict its earlier implication that the invaders frequently raided out of their fortresses 'in full force' supported by the East Anglian and Northumbrian allies. It goes on to say that the armies didn't break out 'more than twice: once when they first landed, before the English force was assembled, and once when they wished to leave those encampments'.

Here Aethelweard's Chronicle is again helpful, because he concedes that this second break-out led the combined Viking force into Wessex proper, including Hampshire and Berkshire. Only after the Vikings had 'devastate[d] the provinces thereabouts' were they confronted, not by Alfred's division, which seems to have missed the break-out, but by Edward's army, which defeated the Vikings at Farnham. But this defeat was by no means the end of the invasion. It was this beaten remnant that the West Saxons besieged on an 'islet' in Buckinghamshire, when their term of service (and provisions) ran out. Even so, the Vikings didn't make their escape, because 'their king had been wounded in battle'. Only when the Northumbrians and East Anglians sent a fleet around to raid the north coast of Devon and Exeter, forcing the bulk of Alfred's relief army to turn west to protect its heartland, was the defeated invading army able to make good its escape, joining up at Benfleet in Essex with Hastein's force, which seems either to have marched there directly from Milton – possibly as a consequence of the negotiations with Alfred that had led to his baptism – or to have proceeded there after slipping away from the Farnham confrontation. This was when Hastein's family was captured, while Hastein himself was out raiding, away from Benfleet, and returned to the Viking chief, so revealing that some earlier negotiation between Alfred and Hastein must have taken place.

So far, neither the burhs nor the king's reforms to the military obligations of Wessex can be seen to have had much positive effect, although the Chronicle claims that 'small bands' of raiding Vikings were pursued 'both from the English army and also from the burhs'. The West Saxons were still capable of defeating a Viking force in the field but not of ejecting the enemy from their kingdom. But as this last war of Alfred's reign progressed, with armies moving and reforming in the east and allies attacking in the west, some signs of the progress in Alfred's defensive tactics begin to emerge. At Exeter, the Chronicle tells us, 'the Danish army had laid siege to the burh' and was unable to break its resistance. When Alfred arrived, the Danes took to their ships. Some flexibility in Alfred's reforms is also evident in the fact that the eastern attackers were now met by a force drawn from 'from every burh east of the [River] Parret, and both west and east of Selwood, and also north from the Thames and west of the Severn, and also some portion of the Welsh people'. Not only could the burhs provide men to confront, and pursue, the eastern Viking army, but Alfred's alliance with the Mercian Aethelred (who had married his daughter, and to whom Alfred had entrusted London, a traditionally Mercian city, when he took it in 886) meant that a combined force of West Saxons and Mercians could pursue the Vikings across the Wessex borders.

This army, commanded by three ealdormen, including Aethelred, finally caught up with them at Buttington in the Welsh borders and forced them into battle, and again defeated them. Even then this persistent and oft-defeated force wasn't finished. It fled back to Essex and mustered again, this

time setting out for Chester and the Wirral, before returning to Essex once again with its spoils, all the time avoid-
ing pursuit. Chester and the Wirral were Mercian targets,
which appear by this time to have come under Anglo-Saxon
(i.e., Ealdorman Aethelred's) control. That Wessex itself had
become too risky to traverse is indicated by the fate of the
fleet that set off from Exeter when Alfred had arrived there.
When the Vikings attempted to raid Chichester, another burh,
manned by 1,500 men according to the Hidage, 'the citizens
put them to flight and killed many hundreds of them, and
captured some of their ships'. The citizens of London were
not so successful when they attempted to confront the eastern
army, which had fortified itself on the River Lea on returning
from its Welsh and Wirral trip. But Alfred himself, having
dealt with the western threat, was able to force them out by
building his own fortresses on either side of the river, compelling the Vikings to abandon their ships and make a dash
across country once again before ending up in Bridgnorth in
Mercia, while the 'English army rode after' them.

The Vikings had had enough. They reached Bridgnorth
in 895, and by the summer of 896 they dispersed, 'one force
going into East Anglia and one into Northumbria'. Though
it would be wrong to say that the heartland of Wessex hadn't
been penetrated (the battle at Farnham and the attack on
Exeter and Devon were all at the core of Alfred's kingdom),
the progress of the war showed that the Vikings came to the
realisation that the pickings were no longer easy there and
restricted themselves to Essex, over the frontier established by
treaty with Guthrum in the 880s, Mercia and Wales. Alfred's
burhs were not an unqualified success; they were unable,
for example, to stop the initial raid digging in, in Kent. The
system would prove its mettle in later years, however, and

it is worth remembering that the Burghal Hidage dates from Edward the Elder's reign. It was in his and subsequent reigns that the burghal system was put to its most effective use in the conquest of what had become known as the Danelaw, where the Vikings had settled from the mid-ninth century. But the relentless, organised way in which the West Saxons and their allies resisted such a serious, multiple invasion in Alfred's reign is in stark contrast to the last-ditch desperation of Athelney and Edington.

The Victorians may have tried to recapture a romantic element to Alfred's last war in their concentration on the story of Hastein's family. The reality, however, is probably better summed up by the dry calculations of the Burghal Hidage. Wessex was to be defended not just by heroism and Christian chivalry, but by 'every hide ... represented by one man, [and] every pole ... manned by four men'.

6

THE KING, THE THIEF, THE CODE
AND THE LETTER:
ALFRED AND THE LAW

Up to now we have concentrated on Alfred and his dealings with the Vikings. As we have seen, the king's reign did not fall neatly into two halves, in the first of which he fought off his enemies and in the second settled down to address himself to more 'peaceful' concerns. The experience of Alfred's last war demonstrates that his kingdom, even as he was expanding its borders, remained under threat throughout. It is perhaps yet another ramification of the story of Alfred and the cakes that, although it shows him in the midst of a military campaign, hell-bent on recovering his realm by force, the actual circumstances are domestic and tranquil. They anticipate the characteristic pose of Alfred the hero-king – reflective, almost other-worldly in the extent of his concern to do right and to have right done to him. So in turning to Alfred at peace, we must bear in mind that Alfred himself is more likely to have seen his obligations as a whole than our tendency to divide them up implies. And for Alfred, and the way he liked to project himself, there were few more important aspects of kingship than the role of law.

The inscription below Count Gleichen's Wantage statue

of Alfred places the king's legal accomplishments second only to his scholarly and educational ones. Alfred, it runs, 'found … the Laws powerless and he gave them force'. The Victorian sculptor was merely continuing a tradition of emphasising Alfred's laws that had been in operation for centuries. Asser mentions Alfred's legal interventions, his law code is collected in an early twelfth-century legal compendium (*Quadripartitus*), and William of Malmesbury, also in the twelfth century, set the tone for successive students of the king when he described Alfred's giving the lie to Cicero's dictum 'laws are silent amid the clash of arms'. Not even the Vikings, William was saying, could put Alfred off lawmaking. William's interpretation of Alfred's administrative legal reforms set in train a strand of thinking of Alfred as the founder of enduring 'original' institutions that inspired generations of Whig historians, who looked as far back as possible for England's 'traditional freedoms', which steady constitutional reform had reinstated.

It is partly because of the general discrediting of such teleological and anachronistic views of the past that Alfred's laws have more recently seemed to play poor relation to his other achievements. More specifically, the legal historian F. W. Maitland (who christened the Burghal Hidage) seemed to have established once and for all that those in search of the origins of the common law should look no further back than the reforms of Henry II. Maitland's cool assessment of the 'forgeries and the fables, legends and the lies' of later writers – in ascribing to Anglo-Saxon law sophistications that the codes themselves were not found to contain – consigned the picture of Alfred as significant lawmaker to legend rather than history.

Yet, as some recent writers have argued, Anglo-Saxon

laws, beginning with Alfred, are worth taking seriously, first for what they can tell us about the state and society they were made in, and then, perhaps, for any signs of continuity to later ages. Not only was Alfred the first Anglo-Saxon king since the seventh-century Ine known to have issued a law code (in Old English, around 695: Offa of Mercia may well have issued one as well, but the best evidence for that is contained in Alfred's own legislation), but there is – relatively speaking – plenty of other evidence that the practice and dispensing of justice was of prime importance to the king. Charters – legal documents that generally record the transfer of land – are not very abundant for Alfred's reign (only seventeen survive that are even attributable to the period: some of those are forgeries, and few are untampered with by later hands). But other documents – including a copy of Alfred's will and a treaty drawn up between Alfred and Guthrum some years after Edington – survive, as do accounts by Asser of the king's hearing an appeal, and, later, by William of Malmesbury of Alfred's making 'laws to familiarise his subjects equally with religious practices and military discipline'. Perhaps most remarkably, there is the 'Fonthill Letter', sent by a Wessex ealdorman to Alfred's successor, his son Edward the Elder, detailing the minutiae of a legal dispute over land, involving theft, cattle rustling and sanctuary seeking. This is a unique snapshot of the day-to-day workings of the law in Alfred's Wessex. It even has a cameo for Alfred himself, to whom the sender of the letter was able to appeal directly. He describes the king standing 'in the chamber at Wardour – he was washing his hands'.

We will turn to the formal legal documents later. But the two most striking instances when Alfred is shown intervening in legal disputes are given by contemporaries, the author of the Fonthill Letter, and Asser, whose picture of Alfred as 'an extremely astute investigator in judicial matters as in everything else' comes almost at the end of his Life, before it breaks off rather suddenly. William of Malmesbury's much later description can be seen to be co-opting quasi-mythical elements to an older, established picture. The Fonthill Letter and, to a lesser extent, Asser's descriptions of Alfred's participation in the legal process allow us to compare his legal reforms in theory and in practice, albeit in a limited way, and bearing in mind that what survives can only represent a small fraction of the legal activity going on in ninth-century Wessex.

THE FONTHILL LETTER

In the final chapter of Asser's book the author describes Alfred sitting 'at judicial hearings for the benefit both of his nobles and of the common people, since they frequently disagreed violently among themselves at assemblies of ealdormen or reeves, to the point where virtually none of them could agree that any judgment reached by the ealdormen or reeves in question was just'. Asser characteristically exaggerates in going on to describe Alfred 'carefully look[ing] into nearly all the judgments which were passed in his absence anywhere in his realm', and the rest of the chapter turns into an illustration of Alfred's preoccupation with the importance of literacy. Asser makes no reference to Alfred's law code, perhaps because it had not been issued when he was writing (around 893), though the dating of the code is not certain. The description of Alfred as a one-man court of appeal may strike us as an idealisation with a deliberately biblical echo, and it is not the only time that Alfred becomes a West Saxon

Solomon. But in the survival of the Fonthill Letter we have some corroborating evidence for Asser's picture of Alfred's personal role in judicial proceedings.

The Letter, generally thought to have been written early in the reign of Edward the Elder, narrates a rather confusing dispute over a portion of land around Fonthill in Wiltshire, a dispute that began in Alfred's reign and dragged on after his death. As the endorsement at the end indicates, this is a document recording the end of the matter, rather than a pleading in an ongoing action. But the way it is couched allows the reader to the follow the convoluted story from the beginning. Frustratingly, we don't know the letter-writer's name, but he was co-opted into the dispute right at the beginning. He tells us of his godson Helmstan, whose claim to Fonthill was first contended after he 'committed the crime of stealing Ethelred's belt'. The man who brought the charge was Aethelhelm Higa, and Higa continued to dispute ownership for some time. The thief Helmstan appealed to his godfather to help him 'prove his right' to the land, which he did first in front of six named men and others 'more … than I can now name'. Higa, for his part, seems to have been bringing the claim because Helmstan's thievery might enable him to show that he had acquired the land by equally dishonest means. The theft of the belt was merely evidence as to bad character, rather than directly related to possession of the land. Since the 'proof' in Anglo-Saxon legal disputes consisted in getting together an impressive enough array of 'oath-helpers' to swear that you had right on your side, Helmstan appeared to have beaten off the claim.

Higa, however, took the matter one stage further. He

would not fully assent until we went in to the king and

told exactly how we had decided it and why we had decided it; and Aethelhelm [Higa] stood himself in there with us. And the king stood in the chamber at Wardour – he was washing his hands. When he had finished, he asked Aethelhelm why what we had decided for him did not seem just to him.

Alfred even indicated that the thief Helmstan should take the oath again, again with the 'helpers'. The second time, with Alfred as witness, the case seemed to have been closed (though Helmstan had, in fact, had to make the land over to the letter-writer, a not entirely godfatherly requirement, we may think, in order to get him to help again, and took it back on a lifetime lease).

But Aethelhelm Higa did not give up easily, and Helmstan's villainous streak gave him another opportunity, when he re-offended shortly after Alfred's death. 'On top of that –', writes our correspondent, 'I do not know whether it was a year and a half or two years later – he [Helmstan] stole the untended oxen at Fonthill … and drove them to Chicklade, and there he was discovered … Then he fled, and a bramble scratched him in the face: and when he wished to deny it, that was brought in evidence against him.' This second offence brought the authorities in. The king's official, a reeve, 'took from him [Helmstan] all the property he owned at Tisbury … He [the reeve] said that he was a thief, and the property was adjudged to the king, because he was the king's man.' As the land at Fonthill was now only held on lease, however, 'he could not forfeit it'. Helmstan managed to wriggle out again, though it is difficult to understand how. He 'sought your father's body'– that is, Alfred's tomb – 'and brought a seal to me', that is, the letter-writer, which, when passed to King Edward, persuaded him to reinstate the recidivist Helmstan: 'you removed his outlawry and gave him the estate to which he has still withdrawn'. It was when the letter-writer succeeded to the land that Aethelhelm apparently tried one last time to claim it. But an appeal to the authority of Alfred's judgement seems eventually to have done the trick: 'if one wishes to change every judgement which King Alfred gave, when shall we have finished disputing?' asks our correspondent, the first recorded invoker of Alfred as legal referee.

The incidentals about this case are almost as intriguing as what is possibly revealed in the main thrust. The glimpse of detective work in the following-up of the bramble scratch on Helmstan's face; the notes of exasperation in the letter-writer's description of the cattle rustling ('on top of that …'); the picture of the busy king dispensing justice not in court but in his bedroom: all these give a picture of life in the reign of Alfred only matched in Asser's always more rose-tinted prose. The historian Alfred Smyth has pointed out that the picture of Alfred may owe something to literary forebears, both in Suetonius' portraits of Roman emperors dispensing justice from their sick-beds or while they put on their shoes, and Einhard's of Charlemagne, also at his wardrobe, giving judgements. But even so (and in which case, it is a good scrap of evidence for Alfred's educational reforms bearing fruit in the wide reading of one of his senior subjects), it is just as likely that Alfred, ever aware of precedent, was emulating imperial models as it is that the picture is a false one.

ALFRED'S CODE

But, apart from its informal nature, at least when the king

became involved, what can the Fonthill Letter tell us about the operation of law in Alfred's time? This is difficult to answer, because we have no way of telling how unusual the case was, and because the details are not entirely clear. What, exactly, was Aethelhelm Higa's claim based on? For that matter, how did the land come into the thief Helmstan's possession in the first place? The letter tells us that Helmstan, when required to prove his entitlement on oath, swore that 'he had it as Aethelryth had sold it into Oswulf's possession at a suitable price', but the connection between either of the claimants to these two is not established. Putting this confusion to one side, how do Helmstan's crimes relate to his title to land?

Here we can bring in Alfred's law code, but if we hope in it to find chapter and verse explaining how theft could lead to forfeiture to another of the king's subjects, we will be disappointed. Alfred's Clause 16 seems to have some bearing on Helmstan's case: 'If anyone steals a cow or brood-mare and drives off a foal or calf, he is to pay a shilling compensation, and for the mothers according to their value.' But no fine is mentioned for Helmstan, while the code makes no mention of possible forfeiture of land. Alfred attached his law code to that of his predecessor Ine, and again Helmstan may seem to be covered by clauses in the old king's code, but again the penalties laid out, from fines to ordeals and mutilation, don't match what happened to Helmstan. Two explanations suggest themselves: the first is that Helmstan, as a man of some property and standing, a 'king's man' himself (i.e., one who had made an oath of loyalty directly to the king) and one with patronage from a man with the king's ear, was able to operate above a level specifically catered for in Alfred's code. This may explain why he made for Alfred's tomb, and why the seal he apparently acquired there offered him some sort of protection. In Ine's code theft is naturally associated with ceorls, freemen of lower status than Helmstan; men of higher status were not thought to be above the law, but the laws they were expected to break were of a different order, and usually to do with political manoeuvring and blood feud.

In his study of Anglo-Saxon lawmaking Patrick Wormald suggests a more radical explanation for the lack of correlation between law code and reality: 'written law was apparently irrelevant'. Certainly, there is no 'reference to a law under which Helmstan is indicted'. But the intervention of the king's official, the reeve, does indicate that something beyond informal meting out of justice was taking place. Wormald proposes a link here, arguing that this intervention was connected to Alfred's law on oaths, 'which turned any criminal behaviour into a breach of fealty, which explains why Helmstan should have forfeit as a "king's man"'. On the face of it, however, Alfred's code stipulates that anyone who breaks his oath is to be imprisoned for forty days, but his possessions return to his keeping at the end of this period. This is rather different from the explanation the reeve gives about seizing Helmstan's property: 'he said he was a thief, and the property was adjudged to the king, because he was the king's man.'

Whether or not Helmstan's case can be indirectly connected to Alfred's code, the fact remains that no clause of it is mentioned. So if everyday disputes could be dealt with separately from the code, what was it for? Here we return almost to the lawgiver of Gleichen's statue: that is, to the primacy of image over substance. All kings, one may assume, settle disputes, but only great ones issue law codes. The first clue

Alfred gives to the tradition he sees himself as following is in the company his law code keeps. As well as appending the code of his great predecessor Ine, Alfred introduces it with extracts and elaborations from the book of Exodus. No other Anglo-Saxon king does this, and it seems typical of Alfred that he should project his ideas back to their biblical source: as in so many things, Alfred's attitude to law seems to have been as much devotional and scholarly as practical. But law is for Alfred a direct result of true religion. And his understanding of the way Christianity and law were first disseminated is echoed in the way he describes the conversion of the Anglo-Saxons in his introduction to the code.

> After it came about that many peoples had received the faith of Christ, many synods were assembled throughout all the earth, and likewise throughout England, after they had received the faith of Christ … they then established … that secular lords might … receive without sin compensation in money for almost every misdeed and offence.

The code does get down to practicalities, of course, as we have already seen from the (apparently ignored) stipulations about cattle compensation. Ine's laws, too, though some of them are replicated or superseded in Alfred's code, lay out schemes for the taking of oaths, punishment of crimes and payment of blood money (*wergild*). But if a new theme can be discerned running through Alfred's laws, it is in his emphasis on lordship, loyalty and the increasing authority and importance of the king. This is most markedly apparent in Alfred's reworking in his introductory remarks of Christ's (and Leviticus') dictum to love thy neighbour: 'he charged everyone to love his lord as himself.' The way this love could best be secured was by oath, and Alfred's first clause of his own code directs that 'each man keep carefully his oath and pledge'. In everyday terms the lines of authority from king through ealdorman and onwards are established, so that Clause 37 demonstrates that everyone serves a lord, even if he is able to transfer allegiance in a sanctioned way. And if a lord is left without proper permission, it is the king who is compensated; the king's authority is further strengthened by the refinement that 'If [the man transferring his allegiance] has committed any wrong where he was before, he who now receives him as his man is to pay compensation for it, and 120 shillings to the king as fine.' This is not a world in which mighty subjects can form private retinues without the king's approval.

Modern historians have pointed out the connection between Alfred's legislation on loyalty and Carolingian forms of oath enforcement, such as Charlemagne's making his subjects over the age of twelve swear fidelity to him as emperor in 802. While Alfred seems to have followed Frankish precedent in various areas of his rule, it is perhaps not too far-fetched to connect this emphasis on loyalty to the king to Alfred's own experiences as well, invoking once more that picture of the unrecognised king embodied in the story of Alfred and the cakes. The narrative sources of the Chronicle and Asser are unsurprisingly vague about the extent of desertion of Alfred's people at the king's lowest ebb, though the Chronicle records that 'the people submitted' to the Vikings in 878, after Chippenham and before Edington. A specific case of desertion by an ealdorman in Alfred's reign, which could have occurred around this time, is recorded in a charter of Edward the Elder, where we learn that an estate being granted 'was originally forfeited by a certain ealdorman, Wulfhere by name, and his wife, when he deserted without permission both his lord King Alfred and his country in spite of the oath which he had sworn to the king and all his leading men'. The scriptwriters of the Alfred film have the king on Athelney noticing a crime wave and resolving to impose law on a lawless people. Of course, the West Saxons already had legislation, much of it dealing with criminal offences. If Alfred's thoughts on Athelney ever turned to legal matters, it seems more likely that legally enforceable loyalty was on his mind.

It would be wrong, however, to give the impression that the contents of Alfred's law code are all a statement of ideals and ideology. If the Fonthill Letter seems to show that the code was not necessarily invoked in practice, it none the less had some very practical clauses. It is difficult to connect the clauses on sword-polishers, or accidental 'transfixing' with a spear (complete with details of the relative height of point and shaft) to anything but their own subject matter. So what were these clauses for? Patrick Wormald's answer is that the code didn't make law so much as 'show what the law [already] was, whether in custom or as the result of royal adjudication or decree'. On this reading Alfred's law code was a picture of a state of affairs, not a document to be consulted practically. The fact that it has survived, and that more ephemeral decrees haven't, both potentially misleads us into assuming it is a document with practical applications and demonstrates the effectiveness of the intentions behind making the code in the first place. It was for posterity, or at least for royal successors to consult before issuing their own codes.

ALFRED'S WILL AND THE TREATY OF WEDMORE

Two more significant legal documents remain from Alfred's reign, both with more obvious practical purpose. One is the remarkable survival of an actual treaty drawn up between Guthrum and Alfred. This can be dated to a four-year period between Alfred's reclaiming of London from the Vikings in 886 and Guthrum's death in 890. Its clauses are an interesting mixture of the political and the legal. First, it sets the boundaries between 'all the English race and all the people who are in East Anglia', 'up the Thames, and then up the Lea, and along the Lea to its source, then in a straight line to Bedford, then up the Ouse to Watling Street'. The treaty is introduced as agreed 'both for the living and the unborn', but political events meant that it was no more than a snapshot: according to its terms, Essex was on the 'East Anglian' – that is, Viking – side, but in 893 the Anglo-Saxon Chronicle mentions, in the context of Alfred's last war, an ealdorman of Essex, implying that control had shifted to the 'English'. The treaty's use of the term 'English race' has been used to strengthen a case for Alfred's unifying ambitions, and the encroachments into Mercia certainly indicate that he looked beyond Wessex's borders. But this was an expansion whose fate was not yet determined. The fact that he put Aethelred, his Mercian son-in-law, in charge of London, which had belonged to Mercia before the Viking invasions, may be a sign that Mercian loyalty to a West Saxon king could not be guaranteed at this stage.

The dating of the treaty to at least eight years after the formal cessation of hostilities marked by the ceremonies at Aller and Wedmore may add something to the case already made for the fragility of Alfred's victory at Edington. The treaty is a document that illustrates a far more secure position on the ground than had obtained in 878. By projecting its vague references to something greater than Wessex forward to a time of a unified England, we risk ignoring the plainer picture, of Alfred at last secure in his territory, able to establish practical ways of working with his former enemy, setting the boundaries of their kingdoms but also agreeing rates of punishment and compensation for the killing of each other's subjects. And it is also perhaps significant that the treaty is made not between Alfred and Aethelstan, the baptismal name Guthrum received as defeated godson in 878, but as Guthrum, the name by which he was known when he almost won Alfred's kingdom for himself. As Aethelstan, he appears to be Alfred's man; as Guthrum, he is his own. We should be wary of placing too much emphasis on this fact: we know that Guthrum issued coinage with his Christian name featured. But it certainly counterbalances the familiar image of the beaten Viking opponent dictated to by the triumphant West Saxon king.

The last legal document from Alfred's reign is a more personal one: the king's will. Again it can be read as a sounding a cautionary note to any portrayal of Alfred as a king whose authority and victorious record allowed him to reign supremely and unquestioned. Concentrating on the king's personal property, the will takes the, to us, unusual step of establishing the way in which the property came to Alfred in the first place, before making arrangements for its disposal at his death. The reason for this is not hard to find. When Alfred succeeded to the kingdom, his older brother Aethelred's sons were far too young to be considered at a time of crisis. But in later years, with the kingdom better established through the king's own efforts, Aethelred's maturing sons might have expected to inherit. As Alfred's own case illustrates, primogeniture was clearly not an established rule in Wessex at this time, so there was no guarantee that Alfred's son Edward should succeed him. But the king's own wishes would be significant, and equally important might be the power base allotted to his offspring from which a claim could be made. So the bequeathing of very significant portions of personal property to Edward and to others in Alfred's direct family, as against the relatively meagre parts assigned to his nephews, would make for a powerful argument in his son's favour at Alfred's death. But references in the will to discussions over the allocation of property, and a dispute at which 'all the counsellors of the West Saxons' were present, demonstrate that this was a complicated matter. And the rebellion of Aethelwold, Alfred's younger nephew, on Edward's succession, shows that Alfred was right to be worried.

The narrative sources, or the king's own writings, do not give this picture of Alfred having to work hard to secure his inheritance. The will even reveals a note of vulnerability to the criticisms of his own subjects, to whom he has to prove his right to dispense property as he saw fit. We hear Alfred pleading with his counsellors, 'I urged them all for the love of me – and gave them my pledge that I would never bear a grudge against any one of them'. Only after a reading of his father's will did Alfred's counsellors agree that 'they could not conceive any juster title' to the land. A twentieth-century novel about Alfred, by Alfred Duggan, makes much of the king's conscience being troubled by the shadow of unfair dealing hanging over his behaviour towards his nephews. It is only in this personal legal document, one of only two wills of Anglo-Saxon kings to survive, that we see signs of Alfred's vulnerability. The law may have made Alfred a Solomon, but it also aided him in the more ordinary task of securing his legacy.

The record of Alfred's legal activities, with its explicit references to his predecessors, shows that the law was hardly 'powerless' when he came to the throne, as the inscription on the Wantage statue has it. Alfred was concerned to project an image of himself as a man of law, but from that we should not necessarily expect to see him as a champion of justice and fair play. The legal world he presided over was one where lordship was the most important bond of all, and legitimacy could in part be established by connecting his own legislation to that of scripture. If the king's own personal experiences at the time of Athelney had demonstrated that, his religious outlook merely confirmed it. Whether issued from a bedroom or written on parchment, law was a way that Alfred strengthened his own position on the throne. Alfred's legal legacy was a strong state with the king indisputably at its head, not 'traditional English liberties'.

7

NECESSARY WISDOM:
ALFRED AS SCHOLAR

More than anything else, Alfred's reputation as a scholar and educationalist places him apart from other Anglo-Saxon kings – we might say, from English royalty in general, as intellectual pursuits have only rarely occupied pride of place at court. If we take Alfred's 'lowest ebb' before Edington, and the stories associated with it, as the defining moment in his career – a moment when the Viking threat was at its most severe and immediate – then the king's later scholarly programme can seem very far removed. We have seen how law need not be treated as a separate case, and how Alfred's law-making was in part a literary activity in which, by anthologising what he took to be the best work of his predecessors (including biblical ones), he laid claim to posterity himself. But with the king's programme of translations, learning and the spread of literacy, we are, on the face of it, entering a different, more tranquil, less threatened realm.

To some extent, of course, that is true. If Alfred had still been fighting directly for his and his kingdom's survival, every other concern would have taken second place, as it must have done when new invaders threatened on occasion after Guthrum's defeat. Alfred himself accepted as much, writing in the preface to one of his translations that his ambitions to spread literacy among 'all the free-born young men now in England' might be accomplished 'provided we have peace enough'. In more complex ways, however, Alfred's scholarly and educational ambitions complement his other activities. A recent historian has argued that the key to understanding Alfred is to see him as an 'integrated' ruler, 'for whom all things were inseparable aspects of his determination to discharge the responsibilities of his high office for the good of his subjects in the service of God'. This view, an echo of another historian's Alfred the 'great all-rounder', which perhaps brings us too close to the 'sports-manlike' Victorian ideal, none the less seems borne out by the king's wholehearted approach to his schemes of translation and teaching.

More than that, what Alfred's programme represents is not just another string to his bow. As the experience of Athelney, and the way it was reworked for public consumption, showed, loss of authority, and of the attributes of kingship, was a fact of Alfred's life in early 878. The only question was whether it would be temporary or permanent. The story of the cakes, and others set at this time, may be no more than colourful illustrations, but they are illustrations of a profound truth: that Alfred's grip on his kingdom was only as secure as he could make it. In the measures he took for the military defence of the kingdom, and the keeping of the peace within it, we can see aspects of his understanding of this point at work. But it is also at work in his enactment of a programme of translation and education. To Alfred a personal interest in wisdom was a facet of true Christian kingship. And the withering away of learning in his kingdom was not a regret-table side-effect of the concentration on defending the realm. It was a root cause of that kingdom's vulnerability to attack,

15. *The Fuller Brooch, dated to the time of Alfred's reign, with the five senses represented by sight (centre), and (clockwise from top left), taste, smell, touch and hearing. Modern scholars have seen this object, together with the Alfred Jewel and others, as representing 'the cult of wisdom at King Alfred's court', to be pursued with all human attributes.*

a 'punishment' for neglect. Alfred understood very well the connection between the nadir of Athelney and the importance of learning. As his translation of Psalms 2:12 put it: 'Embrace learning, lest you incur God's anger and lest you stray from the right path.' His programme to revive learning was a practical as much as a symbolic or spiritual measure.

The picture of Alfred the scholar emerges from the output of translations that survive from the king's court, especially in Alfred's own Prefaces, and from Asser. And as elsewhere, we begin with a story. Asser's recounting of Alfred's childhood victory in the book-learning competition establishes the king's interest in literature from the start. But it is not until the year 887 that Asser describes Alfred as beginning 'through divine inspiration to read and translate at the same time, all on one and the same day'. This miracle is actually just Asser's characteristically over-enthusiastic exaggeration. He has already told us that the king 'remained ignorant of letters until his twelfth year' (rather than his thirty-ninth), and that he was in the habit of 'personally giving, by day and night, instruction in all virtuous behaviour and tutelage in literacy to [his courtiers'] sons'. So in 887 he could already read Old English and even teach others to do so: now he mastered Latin. And as a late learner rather than a refined scholar, Alfred's approach to the idea of education retains a sense of the importance of fundamentals.

Asser expands on the semi-miraculous moment when the king learned to translate Latin, carefully placing himself right at the centre of what he obviously deems the most important aspect of his master's rule. Alfred, he writes, used to get Asser to copy down favoured passages from their reading together into a handbook. It was his desire to read and translate them back to himself that inspired him: 'as soon as that first passage had been copied, he was eager to read it at once and to translate it into English, and thereupon to instruct many others.' The impetus for the king's own scholarly ambitions, as well as his desire to pass on his learning, was thus partly a personal one: 'the pursuit of wisdom' lay at its heart. But Asser shows too that Alfred immediately saw the practical applications of wisdom, telling those senior subjects who failed to follow the king's scholarly example that 'you have neglected the study and application of wisdom', and commanding them to 'apply yourselves more attentively'.

The division of Alfred's programme into two parts,

one concentrating on the spread of literacy, the other on a series of translations into English, should not be allowed to obscure the strong impression that to the king all was subsumed under the category of 'wisdom'. Asser, dwelling on this quality, compares Alfred with Solomon, who 'sought wisdom from God'. But this was no monkish imposition on a simple biographical subject: Alfred's own words in his translations (not least his rechristening of the interlocutors in Boethius's *Consolation of Philosophy* Wisdom and Mind) bear out this preoccupation.

Alfred's inspiration may have been biblical, but it is not surprising to find that here, as elsewhere, his approach to the question of spreading learning is also presented as eminently practical. Alfred never allowed himself to be portrayed too much as the elevated, removed man of contemplation. 'Accordingly, just like the clever bee,' writes Asser, 'King Alfred directed the eyes of his mind far afield and sought without what he did not possess within.' Alfred's own ignorance of Latin was representative of Wessex as a whole, and Latin was the language of learning, as well as of religious authority; so he recruited from outside his kingdom men who could help him. From Mercia came Werferth, bishop of Worcester, Plegmund, whom he later made archbishop of Canterbury, and two less eminent churchmen, Aethelstan and Werwulf. From the Continent Alfred enlisted Grimbald, a monk of St Bertin's Abbey in St Omer, and John 'the Old Saxon'. The last two recruits are a clear reminder that Alfred's mental world was not restricted to Wessex or England but looked out across northern Europe, to some of the places he visited with his father as a child. In fact, Alfred's father, Aethelwulf, had had a Frankish secretary, as well as a Frankish (second) wife, so here again we should be wary of attributing to Alfred an innovation – in this case, willingness to borrow from outside his kingdom – that a predecessor had already introduced.

Lastly, of course, Alfred persuaded Asser to join his court, showering him (according to Asser's own testimony) with gifts, including the grant of two monasteries, 'an extremely valuable silk cloak and a quantity of incense weighing as much as a stout man'. A letter from Grimbald's boss, Fulco, archbishop of Reims, shows that the tactic of combining appeals to spiritual and scholarly righteousness with material offerings was used again by the king. Fulco agrees to send Grimbald to assist in the 'instruction of your people', recognising the goodness of the cause and the claims to universality of the Church, 'for I know that one God is being served in all places'. It has not harmed Alfred's case, however, that his request was accompanied by some 'well bred and excellent' dogs, who fulfil for the archbishop a symbolic as well as a practical role, representing Alfred's desire to keep the wolves of 'the impure spirits who threaten and devour our souls' at bay, just as the dogs will keep away the real wolves 'with which ... our country abounds'.

ALFRED'S CURRICULUM

It was with this team of foreign stars that Alfred set in motion his programme of translations. It is most probably also to this period, around 887, that we should date the beginnings of the compilation of what became known as the Anglo-Saxon Chronicle. The Chronicle is the foundation of most of our knowledge of large tracts of Anglo-Saxon history, and it is unsurprising that such a heavily studied but inscrutable source has inspired numerous theories. Most claims that have been made of the Chronicle – that it was written by Alfred himself, that it is West Saxon propaganda, that it was the fruit of a private enterprise by one of Alfred's ealdormen – have been disputed at one time or another. The usual problem of a lack of surviving original manuscripts is only complicated by the flourishing of copies in the centuries after Alfred's death. Asser's use of the Chronicle in 893 lets us know that a copy existed by then, but it would have taken some time to compile, and it is perfectly reasonable to suppose that it would have formed part of Alfred and his team's scholarly and educational agenda. The Frankish influence of Grimbald may even have played a part in encouraging the West Saxons to create a set of annals to compare with the Annals of St Bertin, a series begun in the 830s at the court of Louis the Pious. Certainly, the unusually detailed accounts of the movements of Vikings on the Continent in the 880s and 890s point to a Frankish influence on the Chronicle for these entries.

If the Chronicle was propaganda, then it was of a very different sort from what we mean by that word today. In one sense Alfred's whole educational programme was propaganda: though there was a strong element of personal interest in it, it was undertaken for the purposes of strengthening his kingdom. But the two elements with which we associate modern propaganda – extreme exaggerations, manipulation and lies; and mass distribution, leading to a collective 'brainwashing' – are absent from the Chronicle and the outpourings of the 'Alfredian renaissance'. As we cannot know how many copies were made of the Chronicle, who wrote it, or for whom it was intended, it is difficult to make any firm statements. It certainly leans towards a West Saxon view of events, but it is in some ways more interesting that Wessex annals should record in any detail what happened outside their kingdom. The Chronicle was written around a time when Wessex was already the last Anglo-Saxon kingdom to be under Anglo-Saxon rule, so it is hardly surprising that Wessex, and Alfred's family, emerge as its central concerns. But as the great Anglo-Saxonist Dorothy Whitelock commented, when replying to an influential article that alleged that the Chronicle exaggerated the straits in which Alfred found himself in 878, 'If the Chronicle was undertaken to enhance Alfred's reputation … the author was very poor at his job'. 'In this period, annalistic writers did not indulge in expansive writing. Still even a writer of annals, if his aim was to paint an enhanced picture of Alfred, might have allowed himself an occasional laudatory adjective or adverb.' In terms of the moment in history around which this book turns, however, it is worth pointing out how relatively expansive is the treatment of the year 878, Alfred's flight to Athelney and his triumph at Edington. There are no cakes in the Chronicle, but the historical setting for the St Neots story is certainly provided. It does not have to be propaganda to recollect in relative tranquillity the moment of greatest danger. From the Chronicle, as much as from Asser, begins the tradition of taking Alfred's experiences on Athelney to represent the low point of his reign.

The difficulty of placing the Chronicle has tended to result in its being treated as a separate case from the rest of Alfred's literary programme, but if it was different, it was surely related. The other, translated, works that emerged from Alfred's court (only the first four are still thought to be largely the king's own work) are: the *Pastoral Care* of Gregory the Great, a handbook for bishops that Alfred saw as applicable to those in secular authority; Boethius's *Consolation of*

Philosophy, a work that would become a medieval staple, a dialogue discussing Fortune and the role of God in our lives; Augustine's *Soliloquies*, a philosophical work to which Alfred seems to have taken the most personal, and freest approach; the first fifty Psalms; the *History* of Orosius, a world history and geography by a pupil of St Augustine that has been credited with providing the inspiration for one of Alfred's military reforms; and the *Dialogues* of Gregory the Great, which contain the pope's Lives of admired saints. Detailed linguistic studies have adjusted this canon (Bede's *Ecclesiastical History* is still the focus of debate, with some scholars including it and others ruling it out) and Alfred's part in it, but although the king's personal involvement is remarkable, discussions of the extent of it shouldn't obscure the more vital point that the programme was Alfred's idea. In a famous passage in the preface to the translation of Gregory's *Pastoral Care*, which is still securely attributed to the king, Alfred explains his purpose in undertaking the programme:

> It seems better to me ... that we too [i.e., as well as Hebrew, Greek and Roman forebears] should turn into the language that we can all understand certain books which it is most necessary for all men to know, and accomplish this, as with God's help we may very easily do provided we have peace enough, so that all free-born young men now in England who have the means to apply themselves to it, may be set to learning (as long as they are not useful for some other employment) until the time that they can read English writings properly.

This was a mission statement, and like most mission statements it was aiming rather high, although Alfred and

16. *The preface to Alfred's translation of the* Pastoral Care, *from the manuscript sent from his court to Werferth, Bishop of Worcester.*

his circle may well have thought that resorting to translation was a major concession. There is no evidence that there was an explosion in general literacy after Alfred's reign, though manuscripts of his translations were certainly distributed. But in the works themselves, their prefaces and the alterations and additions made to them it is possible to see Alfred's preoccupations emerging, so that the works reveal more about his intentions than does any record of their practical effect. If we stay with the preface to the *Pastoral Care*, we can read Alfred's view of the sorry state of learning in his kingdom, and the direct link between this neglect and the invasions of the Vikings: 'Remember what punishments befell us in this world when we ourselves did not cherish learning nor transmit it to other men.' In former times the physical and intellectual treasures of literature, 'wealth and wisdom', were abundant. First, the ability to make use of the wisdom contained in books was lost, then the wealth that went with it was surrendered to invaders, but Alfred makes clear that the trouble started before the Vikings arrived:

Before everything was ransacked and burned ... the great multitude of those serving God ... derived very little benefit from those books, because they could understand nothing of them, since they were not written in our language. It is as if they have said: 'Our ancestors, who formerly maintained these places, loved wisdom, and through it obtained wealth and passed it on to us. Here one can still see their track, but we cannot follow it.' Therefore we have now lost the wealth as well as the wisdom, because we did not wish to set our minds to the track.

If wealth and wisdom were formerly of importance to 'the multitude', it is a different combination, 'warfare and wisdom', that Alfred praises in his description of 'the kings, who had authority over this people'.

17. Top: *The Alfred Jewel, discovered near Athelney in 1693, now in the Ashmolean Museum, Oxford. The inscription translates as 'Alfred ordered me to be made', but the figure may not represent the king. It has been suggested that it shows sight, like the Fuller Brooch, or even that it represents King Solomon, to whom Asser liked to compare his master. Replicas became popular around the time of the millenary, and Unity Mitford even presented one to Hitler.*

Bottom: *The Minister Lovell Jewel, discovered in 1860, might be a smaller version of a similar object.*

The evidence of Alfred's literary programme is enough to demonstrate his interest in wisdom. His recognition of the importance of wealth to his subjects is attested in various places. Asser and Fulco, we have seen, were impressed by the king's generosity. In Bishop Wulfisge's Preface to Werferth's translation of Gregory's *Dialogues*, Alfred is referred to as 'ring-giver', 'Alfred of the English, the greatest treasure-giver of all the kings he has ever heard tell of, in recent times or long ago'. Alfred recognised that churchmen as much as laymen were impressed by material wealth. His translations manifest his spiritual beliefs, but he is also prepared to make practical, material compromises. In his version of Boethius, for example, he even modifies the unequivocal rejection of material goods in the original to concede that it is 'needful' to have 'meat and drink, and clothes, and tools, for the craft you know, which is natural to you, and which is right for you to possess'. Finally, the most famous archaeological arte-fact of Alfred's time, the Alfred Jewel, and its (much smaller) fellows the Bowleaze, Wessex and Minster Lovell Jewels, if they are what most scholars think they are, provide further evidence of his belief in the importance of wealth to accom-pany wisdom. In the Preface to the *Pastoral Care* Alfred men-tions that each copy of the book will contain an *aestel*, worth 50 *mancuses* (in the tenth century 1 *mancus* was the price of an ox, which gives an indication of how valuable these *aestels* were). It is thought that an *aestel* is a sort of pointer to aid public reading; the fittings on the various jewels make it possible that they were intended to be slotted into the top of such pointers, which would account for the *aestel*'s high value. The exquisite work of the Alfred Jewel (on show at the Ashmolean Museum in Oxford), and its possible depiction of the figure of Wisdom, make it an attractive theory that here is a valuable demonstration of wealth to go alongside the treasures of learning.

There has been much discussion of Alfred's picture of the decline of learning 'nowadays' ('there were very few men on this side of the Humber who could understand divine services in English, or even translate a single letter from Latin into English'). It may not have been quite as bad as he painted it, though the writing of charters deteriorates sharply during the period, and Alfred would not have been forced to recruit outside his kingdom if learned men had been available inside it. But even if he exaggerated, this view informed Alfred's approach. He felt that he was starting anew, in an attempt to recover the golden age of learning that he argued had existed in his predecessors' time.

The *Pastoral Care* was, Alfred tells us, to be sent to 'each bishopric in my kingdom', and the survival of one manuscript belonging to Werferth, bishop of Worcester, a member of Alfred's scholarly team, may show that Mercia was included in that formulation by this time. Indeed, for those looking for the origins of a united England in Alfred's time, the references to England as a whole are evidence to place alongside the Chronicle's records of events outside Wessex that Alfred was casting his thoughts beyond the boundaries of his inherited kingdom. The idea of Alfred as founder-king of England, and the objections to it, will be discussed in the following chapter. Here it seems that the shared language is what is being emphasised; and it is hardly surprising that, if Alfred were willing to look beyond his borders for helpers in his revival project, he would be happy for the fruits of their labours to be distributed in their homelands.

The contents of Alfred's programme make his penchant for combining the practical and the symbolic ever clearer.

Alfred tells us that he will not stick to his sources rigidly, translating instead 'sometimes word for word, sometimes sense for sense'. The *Pastoral Care* was a bishops' guide, which Alfred adapted a little to apply even more forcefully to his own case. Where Gregory, for example, writes of the burden of authority, Alfred makes the reference to the burden of teaching. In general, however, Alfred departs less from Gregory than he does from the sources of his other translations. The theme of the proper exercise of rule was one that clearly appealed directly to him. In a sense the dissemination of this book can be seen as a demonstration of Alfred's own commitments as a king, as well as fulfilling its ostensible purpose, to advise bishops on how to tend to their flock.

In his other translations Alfred can be seen making larger changes. In his version of Boethius's *Consolation of Philosophy*, for example, we have seen that he changed the interlocutors in the book's dialogue from Boethius and Lady Philosophy to Wisdom and Mind. If that change represents a personal proclivity for the idea of Wisdom being the paramount virtue, changes in the text itself seem to point towards more outward-looking concerns with kingship. One scholar has pointed out that Alfred's refinements of Boethius and of Augustine's *Soliloquies* put the point of view of the courtier rather than the ruler. A reason for this may be that here, unlike in the *Pastoral Care*, which gives the ruler's point of view, Alfred wanted his courtiers to consider the concerns of authority, both their own and their king's. Loyalty is prized highly: Boethius's book was written in prison, he says, because he was unfairly accused of plotting against his emperor. In Alfred's version the accusation is justified. Boethius was plotting, and even though it was well intentioned, he has to accept the consequences of going against his lord. So the translations help the courtiers to learn loyalty.

In Alfred's Preface to the *Soliloquies* of Augustine, to illustrate his method of learning and translation, he uses the image of a woodcutter gathering wood to build a house. The illustration of intellectual pursuits with practical figures can be seen elsewhere in the work: for example, where ships rather than geometry are used to show how to contemplate divinity. The *Soliloquies* is in some ways the most personal of Alfred's translations, but even so, he adapted it with a practical readership in mind. It was a readership to whom he wished to explain the cares of authority, but also the benefits of loyalty.

THE CASE AGAINST ASSER

The final product of Alfred's literary programme, the creation of one of his most loyal servants, is one with which we are by now most familiar: Asser's book. The possible reasons that Asser undertook the work have already been discussed (see Chapter 1). But it may be instructive to consider something of the book's troubled reputation in later years. Here we move from a picture of Alfred the scholar, attempting to add to the established traditions of learning, to his role in the foundations of scholarship itself. One reason why Alfred's literary programme has assumed such importance in accounts of his achievement may be that those accounts are written up by scholars. Other professionals – for example soldiers (such as John Peddie, in his excellent account of the warrior Alfred) – may take a different view of Alfred's special genius. But Alfred's position as the instigator of and participant in a scholarly enterprise makes him a kind of patron saint of the academy: no wonder that he was invoked as the founder of Oxford University. As the Oxford historian and biographer of Alfred, Charles Plummer, put it: 'surely our hearts may be uplifted at the thought that in all that we do here in the cause of true learning and of genuine education, we are carrying on the work which Alfred left us to do.' And to some scholars the original hagiographer of this patron saint does such a poor job that he cannot be countenanced as the genuine article.

It was V. H. Galbraith, in 1964, who first made a detailed case that Asser was a forgery (though the debate began earlier, in 1841), but his argument seemed to have been convincingly answered by Dorothy Whitelock (again defending Alfred's reputation from those who would rewrite it). The anachronisms he seemed to have discovered, such as Asser's addressing his subject as 'rex Angul-Saxonum', were no such thing: that title, for example, did appear in charters of Alfred's reign. By the time of Keynes and Lapidge's translation of Asser, published in 1983, this debate could be described as a 'horse not yet but nearly dead'. In his monumental biography of Alfred in 1995, however, Alfred Smyth revived the animal and put it through a veritable steeplechase. More anachronisms (towns described before they are likely to have been built up, monastic preoccupations more suited to the late tenth century than a hundred years earlier) and problems with Asser's Latin were put forward, and the work was dismissed as an eleventh-century forgery, written by a monk of Ramsey. More crucially, Smyth argued, Asser was just not convincing. The problem was not that he can be shown to have got the sequence of events wrong, or that he misplaces or misdates his material: for Smyth, Asser simply gets Alfred himself wrong. We will turn to the question of Alfred's 'character' and its historical fortunes in more detail in the following chapter. But for Smyth, Asser's dwelling on the king's infirmities and 'nails of many tribulations' hardly seems to fit the man who so vigorously fought for, defended, taught and expanded his kingdom. Smyth revives the case against Galbraith's 'neurotic invalid' Alfred, recoiling from a man who, on the evidence of Asser, has been diagnosed with a 'catalogue of disagreeable disorders'. All this, Smyth argues, was perpetrated to create a sanctified picture of the king, an early medieval saint whose physical sufferings had to be on display to inspire reverence.

The argument is presented, and was received, in histrionic terms, more reminiscent of a cinema poster than an academic debate. Asser is the 'Battleground of Scholarship, Charnel House of Scholars'; Smyth's case was later dismissed as 'preposterous', and 'a terrifying demonstration of [the] dangers' of not having 'sufficient knowledge of Latin'. The result was a technical knock-out in favour of Smyth's opponents. Asser's Latin was effectively defended on linguistic grounds, and it was convincingly demonstrated that the Ramsey monk couldn't have written it. The case against Smyth's suggested forger certainly seemed to be proved, but just because Smyth appeared to have got the wrong man, that does not mean that Asser's work itself was in the clear. True, no convincing proof of an anachronism had survived, but Asser may still be thought too whimsical to be genuine. Smyth even argued that Archbishop Parker's inclusion of the cakes story was further evidence that the rest of Asser was equally unreliable: '[T]here is no need to treat it [i.e., the cakes story] as a significantly different tradition in the development of the Alfred myth from, say, the tale of Alfred's winning of the book prize from his mother.'

The best recent defence of Asser's idiosyncrasies comes from a scholar writing outside the academy, Michael Wood, who, perhaps because of his distance from the academic world that to some small extent Alfred had a hand in creating, is able to make a measured case set in wider historical context. For all its oddness, Wood argues, Asser's version of Alfred 'can be made to yield a convincing psychological picture'. But, as we have seen throughout this book, and as Wood acknowledges in his essay, the 'genuine' Alfred is likely to be irrecoverable. So Asser's portrait does not have to be correct, or even convincing, for his work to be real. On the contrary, its whimsicality can be taken as evidence in its favour. If Asser reads oddly, that is because he is writing in a genre as yet unformed. His hagiographical slant, even down to the personal physical tribulations he puts Alfred through, may or may not be an accurate picture of Alfred, but there is no need to believe that a ninth-century monk writing a biography of a living king *wouldn't* write it in this way. Ultimately, the best argument in favour of a genuine Asser, apart from the absence of a 'smoking gun' that would show it *can't* be real, is that it is so strange and so difficult to fake. No forger cunning enough to be familiar with ninth-century Welsh place-names and the inner workings of Alfred's court seems likely to emerge.

Modern scholars tend to emphasise that their renditions of Alfred are done in specifically ninth-century colours, but the argument over Asser demonstrates something different: that it is difficult to be sure we're looking at ninth-century colours when we see them. In seeking to remove the perennially sick, troubled and poorly educated Alfred from the picture, as well as one for whom (as we will see in the next chapter) sex was a source of guilt and shame, the anti-Asser party is imposing a twentieth-century sensibility on its ninth-century subject. It is easy for a modern reader to take nineteenth-century or earlier views of Alfred with a large pinch of salt: when Arthur Conan Doyle tells us that Alfred's aim was that 'every boy and girl in the whole of the nation should be able to read and write', we know that he is writing more for his own time than ours. But equally, when Asser's 'neurotic' Alfred is dismissed, and a resolute 'all-rounder' is put in his place, with a keen eye for the uses of propaganda and an understanding of the benefits of co-operation with European 'partners', we should acknowledge the likelihood that this too may be a contemporary imposition on a ninth-century subject. Asser may be frustrating, and Alfred's own writings may seem to give us more genuine glimpses of the king's personality, but the public and private Alfred are likely to have been 'integrated' too. Whichever way we look at him, we are looking through our own sensibilities. And however sophisticated those are, they are still eleven centuries removed from Alfred's, and from Asser's.

Wessex's experience in 878 had taught Alfred that a kingdom's survival and strength depended on many things. A scholarly programme was certainly part of his answer, and learning obviously appealed to Alfred personally. The fact that no other English king attempted such a thing makes Alfred's achievement in this endeavour all the more impressive. Perhaps, as a fifth son, Alfred had once been intended for the Church, and for the scholar's life. But we need to be mindful that Alfred was still a king among scholars, not a scholar who happened to be a king.

8

THE SICK MAN'S PRAYER: A
PERSONAL ALFRED

For centuries part of the appeal of King Alfred has been the impression that we could know not only what he did but also what he was like. When Alfred's millenary was celebrated in Winchester in 1901 (Alfred was widely thought at the time to have died in 901, not 899), Lord Rosebery gave a speech to the crowd that made the point explicitly. At the unveiling of Hamo Thornycroft's massive statue Rosebery explained that the 'secret' of Alfred's 'hold on the imagination of mankind' was 'in the first place, a question of personality. He has stamped his character on the cold annals of humanity.' E. A. Freeman, writing at the height, rather than the end, of the Victorian period, also thought that Alfred's perfection was to be found in his 'character', which combined, in the historian's view, all the best qualities of a man and a ruler, and which he was able to compare, with quasi-scientific authority, with that of other 'greats': St Louis, William the Silent, George Washington, all of whom, of course, fell just short.

The idea of Alfred as a 'perfect character' was not an original one. In his *History of Great Britain* (1754–62) David Hume had described him as 'the model of that perfect character, which, under the denomination of a sage man, philosophers have been fond of delineating, rather as a fiction of

18. *Lord Rosebery at the unveiling of Hamo Thornycroft's statue at the Winchester Millenary. The lectern in the shape of a lyre is probably meant to remind the audience of the king's minstrel experiences. Thornycroft is the white-haired man standing on the left, behind the mortar-boarded bishops of Winchester and Salisbury.*

their imagination, than in hopes of ever seeing it really existing'. For a long time Alfred was not just a 'mirror for princes' – an example to rulers – but a model for all to emulate. In Dickens's *A Child's History of England*, he is 'the noble king who, in his single person, possessed all the Saxon virtues … As it is said that his spirit still inspires some of our best English laws, so, let you and I pray that it may animate our English hearts.'

In recent years we might expect the more rigorous approach, which has, among other things, consigned the story of the cakes to myth, to have put considerations of Alfred's character to one side. What is true for Alfred's public achievement, that 'we hold that Alfred was a great and glorious king in part because he tells us he was' – in other words, that Alfred wrote or supervised nearly all the literary sources of information about himself – applies even more forcefully for the private Alfred. At least there is some corroboration, from archaeology, and those literary sources not produced under the king's nose, for Alfred's deeds. For his person we are almost completely reliant on his authorised biographer and the king's own writings. None of this material is 'private', and image-making is not a modern phenomenon. That observation has become easy enough to accept for later public figures, from Elizabeth I to Napoleon, but it is true too for an early medieval king such as Alfred. The sophistication of the techniques may alter over time, but the core idea that a private image can be fashioned for public consumption is at work in Alfred's age as well. This is not to argue that Asser, the Chronicle or Alfred's translations give a deliberately false impression, but to be aware that their portrayal of Alfred and his world-view is to some degree what Alfred wanted to make known. Whatever conclusions we can draw from the sources for Alfred's private life must always be heavily qualified.

All this, however, has not stopped modern observers from trying to reconstruct a personal Alfred. One reason for this, at least in popular renditions, may be a reaction against the Victorian 'perfect' Alfred. Less than seventy years after the millenary commemorations the sturdy, assured, Victorian-style king of Thornycroft's Winchester statue or Rosebery's speech was replaced for popular consumption by a comparatively unrecognisable celluloid

19. David Hemmings as Alfred, 1969. The film Alfred the Great *combined a cavalier approach to history with gestures to archaeological authenticity. The sword is based on the Abingdon sword, a find from the period, and the lettering adapts the words of the Alfred Jewel to show that this weapon was made for Alfred's father Aethelwulf.*

version. For all its anachronisms this interpretation was clearly an attempt to reclaim something of the 'genuine' early medieval Alfred from Victorian romancers. The film Alfred of 1969, with David Hemmings in the title role, was memorably described by the critic Pauline Kael as 'some sort of sword-swinging pacifist with a Gandhian anti-sex, self deprivation twist'. This 'confused' Alfred, reluctant to succeed to the throne (as Kael asked, 'was there ever a hero-king on screen who wasn't reluctant?'), troubled on it, has taken over in popular portrayals. In a recent novel the sexual hang-ups are still there, together with a rather pathetic portrayal of the king's gastric complaints (the film restricts reference to these to Hemmings's occasionally growling, 'it gives me gut's-ache!'). And if we compare a recent children's history, where readers are warned that Alfred's hand in all the sources that survive makes them untrustworthy, with Dickens's inspirational spirit, the debunking picture seems complete.

In fairness, for all its risibility in other respects, the Hemmings Alfred is much closer to Asser's king than is the Victorian paragon. And while modern scholars may have been more circumspect about reconstructing the king's character from such skewed origins, they too have felt the necessity of replacing the 'perfect' Alfred with a more flawed, credible model. In spite of Asser's shortcomings, the existence of his biography, as well as of Alfred's own writings, still seems to offer the chance to glimpse a 'personal' Alfred. One recent scholar, for example, admits to finding Alfred 'maddeningly professorial'.

Asser explicitly set out to describe his subject's 'life, behaviour [and] equitable character', and he remains the most influential illustrator of the 'personal' Alfred, for good and ill. His work has been described as reading 'like the school report which every schoolboy would like to write about himself'. But other historians have pointed out those elements of Asser's work that make it more likely that a schoolboy would want to lose the report on his way home.

Asser's Alfred may be wise, and diligent, and good, but he is emphatically not perfect.

Part of the reason that some historians have wanted to reject the work of Asser, as we saw in the previous chapter, is their difficulty in accepting the personal picture he paints. This simple emotional distaste for Asser's Alfred can become buried under the more technical arguments against him. Much of the focus of those who would discredit Asser is trained on his methods and the way the book is constructed. But even putting these objections to one side, can there be any point in taking seriously the largely uncorroborated and confused testimony of a single, biased witness to the personal qualities of a king who died eleven centuries ago?

The question is certainly not answered by accepting Asser as genuine. You do not have to think Asser is a forgery to doubt what he says, particularly about the king's personal life. We have seen that Asser can be inconsistent, as about Alfred's learning to read, or frustratingly elliptical, as when he doesn't bother to tell the reader the name of Alfred's wife, the Mercian noblewoman Ealhswith, while describing the wedding feast and giving the name of his mother-in-law. When he comes to the king's character and personal habits, Asser paints a picture that is, superficially, part conventional and part peculiar. It would surprise no one to read Asser's laudatory descriptions of a vigorous and pious king,

> pursuing all manner of hunting; giving instructions to all his goldsmiths and craftsmen as well as to his falconers, hawk-trainers and dog-keepers; making to his own design wonderful and precious new treasures ...; reading aloud from books in English and above all learn-

ing English poems by heart ... He was also in the invariable habit of listening daily to divine services and Mass.

This picture, while hardly 'warts and all', seems unremarkable: a favourable portrait by a loyal subject that actually reveals little inner life. Alfred was a warrior with a demonstrable interest in learning and a strong faith. Gifts and treasure were a crucial tool for a king in securing his followers' loyalty, so it is no wonder to find Alfred showing an interest in them, and we have seen how in his own writings Alfred squared an interest in material goods with Christian belief. Again, proficiency and interest in hunting were the normal attributes of kings. And Alfred's love of English books is consistent with his own literary activities as well as with Asser's picture of the king's childhood.

Strangely, given the sceptical tendencies noted above, this conventional part of Asser's depiction of the personality of the king has not attracted much debunking. But elsewhere Asser gives other, apparently odder, insights into the king's personal life, and it is these that have been found harder to take. Asser's Alfred is unwell, chronically so. Throughout his biography there are references to Alfred's 'illnesses' and 'infirmities', but at two stages Asser goes into more detail. Two days after his wedding, Alfred 'was struck without warning in the presence of the entire gathering by a sudden severe pain that was quite unknown to all physicians'. This pain continued, Asser writes, 'without remission, from his twentieth year up to his fortieth and beyond' – that is, up to the time Asser is writing. Nor was this Alfred's first long-term affliction. Previously, he had suffered the 'particular kind of agonising irritation' of piles 'from his youth'.

ALFRED AND SEX

This Alfred is the 'neurotic invalid' that some historians have found impossible to believe in. In particular, the warrior-king of the Chronicle seems far distant from the man 'rendered virtually useless', in Asser's words, by his afflictions, or even by the dread of their recurrence ('his fear and horror of that accursed pain would never desert him'). So it is the flaws in the image of Alfred, rather than the unlikely perfections, that arouse suspicion. The testimony from sources other than Asser is not conclusive, though it may be suggestive. The reference in the third-person preface of Alfred's translation of Boethius, for example, to the 'various and multifarious worldly distractions which frequently occupied him in mind and body', may be taken as referring to illness, but it may be more significant, once we look at Asser's own account of the course of Alfred's afflictions more closely, that the 'bodily' distractions can also be taken to refer to lust.

Some investigators have tried to make a medical diagnosis of Alfred's long-term illness from Asser's unscientific references, the most popular now being that Alfred suffered from Crohn's disease, a chronic inflammation of the small intestine, although as the disease is described in medical literature as 'difficult to diagnose' and easy to confuse with other diseases, the diagnosis of a ninth-century patient based on the vague testimony of a biographer seems a little hazardous. But Asser's explanation of Alfred's health difficulties and his description of the course of Alfred's illnesses go to the core of the version of Alfred that he (and Alfred himself?) was trying to present and give a clue to the difficulties later readers have had with this Alfred.

To understand more, we have to examine the reasons that Asser gave for Alfred's sufferings. He considers others' suggestions, which indicate that the king's 'infirmities' were widely known about and discussed (or, at least, that Asser wanted to give the impression that was the case): 'Many, to be sure, alleged that it had happened through the spells and witchcraft of the people around him; others, through the ill-will of the devil, who is always envious of good men; others, that it was the result of some unfamiliar kind of fever; still others thought it was due to the piles.' Asser appears to be moving from the supernatural (spells, witchcraft and the devil) to the medical (complications of an 'unfamiliar fever', or of the king's known affliction with piles). The story he goes on to tell, however, though it is superficially connected to the last suggestion, that Alfred's long-term illness was a consequence of his existing medical complaint, relates back to the supernatural explanations that as modern readers we instinctively put to one side.

Alfred, 'on a previous occasion' – that is, some time before his marriage – had made a detour on a Cornish hunting trip to a saint's shrine, where he prayed

> for a long while in order to beseech the Lord's mercy, so that Almighty God in his bountiful kindness might substitute for the pangs of the present and agonizing infirmity [i.e., piles] some less severe illness, on the understanding that the new illness would not be outwardly visible on his body ... [S]hortly thereafter – just as he had asked in his prayers – he felt himself divinely cured from that malady.

The 'substitution' of the requested replacement illness arrived only after Alfred's wedding day. The timing of that seems to become significant, at least to a reader of modern sensibilities, when Asser goes on to explain the origins of Alfred's first illness, piles. As an illustration of the 'kindly disposition of [Alfred's] mind towards God', Asser recounts how Alfred found himself 'unable to abstain from carnal desire', and prayed that God 'would more staunchly strengthen his resolve in love of His service by means of some illness'. God obliged: 'he contracted the disease of piles through God's gift'. In relating Alfred's first illness to sexual desire, Asser makes the connection between sex and the second illness, contracted 'at his wedding feast', all but explicit.

Michael Wood, in his essay on Asser, takes the biographer's 'psycho-sexual' explanation seriously, relating it to a passage in Alfred's translation of Boethius in which the king wrestles with the problem of 'the evil desire of lust'. Wood uses this argument as evidence for a 'genuine' Asser, showing how, to a medieval sensibility, 'illness and pain had meaning'. Of course, those who argue that Asser is a forgery also propose a medieval, if not a contemporary, date for authorship, so evidence of the same 'monkish' sensibilities is not necessarily evidence for a genuine Asser. But it is certainly an argument in favour of a believable picture of Alfred.

Perhaps it is this Alfred, wrestling with the 'problem' of sex, rather than the idea of a sick Alfred that has remained so off-putting to some scholars. Asser portrays the king as overcoming his infirmities, after all, and there is nothing inconceivable medically about a man with a long-term but sporadic illness (such as Crohn's disease) leading an active life, punctuated with episodes of pain and difficulty. There is even a scrap of evidence from another source to suggest that Alfred sought far afield for a cure, though we shouldn't put too much emphasis on it. In an Anglo-Saxon medical compilation known as Bald's Leechbook there are some remedies for afflictions such as piles, and at the end of this section is the note, 'All this the Lord Patriarch of Jerusalem ordered to be told to King Alfred'. Asser mentions that the patriarch corresponded with his master ('I have even seen and read letters sent to him with gifts from Jerusalem by the Patriarch Elias'). It is hardly conclusive, but if we accept that Alfred appears to have requested a remedy from Elias, then he took his affliction seriously; it lends more credibility to Asser's portrayal.

Alfred's conviction that sexual desire, prayer and illness were all related is perfectly credible in the world of faith he inhabited. We don't know why he was ill, though it seems foolish to doubt that he was, merely because he led an active life. It certainly seems believable that Alfred thought he was ill because he had prayed to be. Other prayers, even more dramatic, to rid his country of the Vikings, had been answered. Of course, Asser's portrayal of Alfred, illness and sex has the heroic quality of myth, at least in Alfred's patient suffering of it, and it certainly seems exaggerated ('He does not even have a single hour of peace'). But if we doubt Asser because he constructs a 'neurotic' king, we allow our twenty-first century prejudices to interfere with our judgement just as much as Freeman and Co. were influenced by theirs.

Indeed, if we look at the historiographical fortunes of the portrayal, or lack of it, of Alfred, women and sex, they can be taken almost as a barometer of the way the king's reputation has been adapted to prevailing views over the centuries. If in his own time, sex could be referred to, at least to be castigated, as a sin, it subsequently disappears altogether, only to resurface in almost comically archetypical fashion for later ages. So not only Asser but also the eleventh-century Life of St Neot that is the earliest source for the cakes story mentions the youthful Alfred's struggles with 'licentiousness'. Women figure little in Asser's account, but any extended treatment is usually negative. He tells the story of Offa of Mercia's daughter Eadburh, who married an eighth-century predecessor of Alfred's, becoming queen of the West Saxons, a title she abused so heinously that 'as a result of her very great wickedness, all the inhabitants of the land swore that they would never permit any king to reign over them who ... invited the queen to sit beside him on the royal throne'. This story is told in the context of Judith, Alfred's stepmother, who on Alfred's father's death married his brother, an action that again invites Asser's censure (though it is Alfred's brother, rather than his stepmother-turned-sister-in-law, who is criticised).

The shorter treatments of later medieval writers ignore Alfred and sex, as does Foxe's portrayal of a purely public Alfred in his *Book of Martyrs*. In the seventeenth century Alfred was invoked as an almost purely political animal, but by the eighteenth century he began to become more generally fashionable again, and there are romantic if not sexual elements in portrayals of a fantasy hero-king (albeit with some fairly overt contemporary political overtones) in works such as Sir Richard Blackmore's epic twelve-volume verse *Alfred* (1723), Thomson and Mallet's *Alfred: A Masque* (1740) and John Home's *Alfred: A Tragedy* (1778). The author of this last felt compelled on its first printing to answer critics of the staged version, who had complained that 'the Hero, the Legislator, is degraded to a Lover, who enters the Danish camp from a private, not a public, motive, and acts the part of an impostor' – that is, in order to rescue his beloved rather than to assess the enemy's capabilities. Here, of course, historically pedantic critics were insisting on the correct version of a story that only gained currency over 200 years after the king's death.

By the nineteenth century, however, an active repression of all sexual matter relating to Alfred had set in. In the Jubilee edition of *The Whole Works of King Alfred*, for example, printed in 1852, only the first ten chapters of the translation of Gregory's *Pastoral Care* are included. The reason given is not only that these chapters 'are sufficient to shew the character of the work'. 'Even if it were desirable to translate the whole, a great impediment to our doing so would be the nature of some parts of it, far too indelicate for more modern general perusal, though quite of a piece with other treatises of the time.' Among the other matters discussed in the omitted chapters – and it is hard to conceive of anything else that this prim reference can be applied to – are Gregory's (and Alfred's) fairly detailed discussion of the perils of sexual lust. The fact that, with St Paul, the author and translator abhor sexual pleasure ('let those who have wives be as if they had none') seems to matter less to the Jubilee editors than the very association of the king with sex. In this period the role of women in any memorialisation of Alfred became purely decorative. At Alfred's Winchester millenary, tableaux depicting scenes from Alfred's life were enacted, including one of 'Saxon women attending the wounded' after the Battle of Ashdown, which depicted the women of Wessex as nuns – pristine, heavily wimpled and angelic.

This puritanical streak did not entirely disappear with the rise of the more scientifically minded historical approach, however. Charles Plummer's first 'modern' biography of the king (1901) still gets hot under the collar that 'modern writers should lend even half an ear to the wretched tales' of Alfred's early 'licentiousness', contained in the Life of St Neot. This fastidiousness over sexual matters persists later into the twentieth century and may be said to play at least

20. *Among those ministering to the wounded after Ashdown in this Winchester re-enactment are members of Mayor Bowker's family. All the tableaux were 'admirably arranged by Mrs Scott': despite the grand ambitions and exalted guest list, the Winchester Millenary retained much of the quality of a local church fete.*

some part in the debate over Asser's genuineness from the beginning. Even Asser's defenders seem slightly squeamish over Alfred and sex. Asser's first modern editor, W. H. Stevenson, described Asser's references as repellent, and Dorothy Whitelock found them wearisome. (Whitelock's printed version of Alfred's laws in her *English Historical Documents*, vol. 1, jumps from clause 10 to clause 12; clause 11, a note tells us, 'is concerned with compensations for assaults of various kinds and in various circumstances against women'; even the Jubilee edition doesn't shy away from mentioning what punishment should be meted out 'if a man take hold of a churlish woman's breast'.)

One consequence of desexualising Alfred and his world

has been to make him a perfectly unthreatening children's role model. The unblemished good soul that Dickens described for children would crystallise in the twentieth century into the West Saxon headboy-king of portrayals in R. J. Unstead or the Ladybird series. The same purity still holds good in later popular portrayals for an older readership. Alfred Duggan, whose novel *The King of Athelney* was published at the beginning of the 1960s, makes Alfred's wedding-feast illness into a crippling attack of shyness and interprets Asser's mention of Alfred's mother-in-law and neglect of his wife to mean that Alfred preferred the former to 'value as a friend'. This Alfred's wedding night passes off 'fairly well', without hint of self-searching or of previous 'experience'.

Duggan's is perhaps the last hurrah of the stiff-upper-lip Alfred, but the barometer was about to shift, and, sure enough, popular versions of the king's sex life shifted too. In the film *Alfred the Great* the Viking invasions are practically a sub-plot to the love triangle formed between the repressed, misogynistic Alfred, Prunella Ransome's liberated Ealhswith ('I am proud as well. Must I be humble?') and Michael York's hair-tossing free-spirited Guthrum. This Alfred rapes his new wife, admitting 'lust is a plague to me', while it is Guthrum who, when Ealhswith is exchanged as a hostage, introduces her to a world of sexual fulfilment. (Ian McKellen, who played 'Roger the Bandit', a fictional companion of Alfred on Athelney, has reminisced that his character's wife, played by Vivien Merchant, received some unusual advice from her famous husband when he visited the set. He 'told Vivien that she was not to speak any of the unspeakable lines in the script, so the director agreed that her part would be mute'. This is the extent of Harold Pinter's part in Alfred's afterlife.) The tide turns at the Battle of Edington, when a squadron of fighting women make an unexpected appearance. What would the Revd Charles Plummer have made of it?

This late 1960s' version of the 870s – a combination of a ninth-century *Barbarella* with, in the battle scenes, *The Benny Hill Show* – surprisingly bears some relation in its details to earlier fictional re-creations, as well as relaying faint, garbled echoes of Asser's troubled Christian and Alfred's own prot-estations of reluctance to take the throne in his translation of Boethius. William of Malmesbury's story of Alfred dis-guised in the Viking camp before Edington becomes in this film a daring raid to recapture the king's family from Guthrum. But in that detail, at least, the film follows John Home's *Alfred: A Tragedy*, of 1778. Once again we see how the stories about Alfred persist, allowing fictional elbow-room for his character and time to be adapted to any age. In Bernard Cornwell's recent Alfred novel the king's sexual hang-ups are frankly referred to, again to be unfavourably compared with the unrepressed Vikings, who find Alfred's soul-searching amusing.

THE PRACTICAL KING

There are less historiographically and mythically fraught aspects of the personal Alfred that still seem to offer glimpses of his character. But, as with the areas of sickness and sex, Alfred the man is not easy to divorce from Alfred the king. The idea of a public and private sphere had much less meaning for Alfred's time than for ours: this is why Alfred's translations so seamlessly conflate the discussion of leading the good life with being a good ruler. And we have seen how, even when he was washing his hands in a private chamber,

Alfred was ready to do a king's work. We have also seen on how many fronts – military, political, religious, educational – he approached the task of consolidating his victory over the Vikings, and in some ways that seems the best indicator of the nature of his character. Alfred saw the practical applications of almost every endeavour; for him the most practical undertaking for any human being was one many modern observers would see as outside the considerations of everyday life: that is, coming closer to God.

Alfred uses a metaphor of house-building, for example, in his Preface to Augustine's *Soliloquies*, in order to describe his attempts 'to be useful here and likewise to arrive there', i.e., in heaven. Here the practical and the eternal co-exist side by side in the king's world-view. This interest in building seems more than metaphorical, however. Asser tells us that Alfred commanded 'royal residences of masonry [to be] moved from their old position and splendidly reconstructed at more appropriate places'. None of Alfred's 'splendid' reconstructions survives, though there are vestigial traces of his reconstruction of Winchester and London, which demonstrate a planned approach to town development, not just the expediency of defence measures. But with its technical references to 'staves and props and tie-shafts, and handles of each of the tools that I knew how to work with', Alfred's description of house-building seems to indicate a more direct familiarity with more humble manual labour than mere royal overseeing and plan-drawing. Inevitably, the words return us to that moment of greatest distress in his reign, to Athelney in 878, where, Asser and the Chronicle tell us, 'King Alfred, with a few men, made a fortress'.

The practical man who sees in 'every tree … something for which I had a need at home' is the abiding personality that both Asser and Alfred himself reveal. Asser makes Alfred an inventor too, famously ordering a candle clock to be made in order to divide his day more accurately. Whether or not Asser has the details right (it has proved almost impossible for anyone to replicate the candle clock as he describes it), the picture of an almost obsessive need to squeeze every- thing out of the time available to him in no way contradicts the public Alfred. Vigorous, reflective, practical and trou- bled, Alfred the man mirrors Alfred the king. At the core is the Christian, and any attempt to get close to the 'real' Alfred must accept that fact. Alfred dedicated his life to God, to dis- covering 'the most direct way to the eternal home and to eternal glory and to the eternal rest which is promised to us', as he put it in the Preface to the *Soliloquies*, but he conceived of an almost infinite number of ways to do that.

9

THE FOUNDING FATHER

In 1841, four years into the reign of the new queen, a Fine Arts Commission was appointed to oversee the decoration of the new Palace of Westminster. Charles Barry and Augustus Pugin had been commissioned to replace the buildings destroyed by fire in 1834, and artists were now invited to submit works on an English historical or an English literary theme. In the next few years several competitions were held for different media. For the oil painting section in 1847, the thirty-year-old George Frederic Watts offered *Alfred Inciting the Saxons to Prevent the Landing of the Danes by Encountering them at Sea*. This massive work, mostly executed in Florence and which now hangs in a Committee Room in the House of Commons, is Anglo-Saxon history painting under the influence of the Renaissance masters. In fact, Watts's Italian travels had been made possible by his winning an earlier prize, in the competition for 1843, for a painting on the subject of the British chief Caractacus being led as a captive through the streets of Rome. That subject had not met with universal critical approval, however; it was felt that works celebrating national history should not dwell on a defeat.

Watts's reasons for choosing Alfred seem to have been a combination of personal inclination and political decision. He wrote privately of his identification with the character of

21. This detail from G. F. Watts, Alfred Inciting the Saxons to Resist the Landing of the Danes by Encountering them at Sea, *1847, shows the king as a youthful superhero, pointing out the path to Imperial naval glory.*

a king who suffered from a 'misery and despondency' that the artist also felt keenly. But the Alfred that Watts chose to depict is anything but the invalid king we observed in the previous chapter. He is the youthful captain, leading from the front, pointing with his sword, 'an Apollo' in Watts's words, haranguing his followers. The contemporary catalogue note to the picture makes it clear that Watts has a specific version of the historical Alfred in mind too, beyond the vigorous warrior. 'In an interval of truce, Alfred's mind conceived of an idea which may be looked upon as the embryo of the naval glory of England.' If some subjects, such as Caractacus, could arouse disagreement among critics merely by the decision to paint them, Alfred was secure as the originator of what the Victorians took to be the foundations of English greatness: a united England itself, the Navy, a constitutional monarchy, even the empire. For all his personal appeal to the artist as a troubled individual, it is Alfred's institutional adaptability that made him such an ideal subject for Victorian public art, even before the celebration of his millenary made him fashionable to the point of ubiquity. As well as depicting the king as a proto-Nelson for parliamentary viewers, Watts placed Alfred in another composition, a fresco of *Justice: A Hemicycle of Lawgivers*, done for the New Hall at Lincoln's Inn. In that work Alfred takes his place alongside Moses, Zoroaster and Minos. Even to a single artist Alfred could embody more than one aspect of England's foundations.

Alfred's reputation as multiple founder offers a more conventional way of looking at the king, whom throughout this book we have been glimpsing at first through the prism of story, narrative and anecdote. Tracing English institutions and traditions back to Alfred is a quasi-historical game that has been played for centuries. Modern scholarship has discredited most of these shaky genealogies, but, however specious, some of them retain power in part because they seem to show a more 'serious' link between later ages and the past. More reliably, however, these pseudo-historical notions illustrate the concerns of the time in which they originate or become established, which is rarely Alfred's.

ALFRED RULES THE WAVES

By the nineteenth century, for example, it seems to have been generally accepted that Alfred was, as Watts imagined him, the father of the British Navy. That identification ultimately rests on a few references to Alfred's sea battles and his part in ship design in the Chronicle. It was not often mentioned that those ships met with limited success, particularly in 896, the year that Alfred is credited with devising new vessels, capturing some of the enemy off the Isle of Wight but allowing others to get away because the West Saxons had run aground. Of course, Anglo-Saxons had been seafarers long before Alfred. One need only think of the most famous archaeological remnant of Anglo-Saxon England, the seventh-century ship burial at Sutton Hoo. Shortly after Alfred was born, his eldest brother Aethelstan, as under-king of Kent, captured nine Viking ships in 851. It may be significant that Asser, as well as one version of the Chronicle, omits the phrase 'fought in ships' for their description of Aethelstan's naval engagement, making Alfred's sea battles (some of which preceded 896, the 'embryonic' year for the Royal Navy) seem more innovative. Major naval engagements remained extremely rare throughout the medieval period, and until the Spanish Armada of 1588 it was very unusual for any serious fighting to take place at sea.

22. Alfred Bowker thought it 'impossible to compare the new cruiser with the old Anglo-Saxon craft', but the makers of the invitation to the launch of HMS King Alfred had a go.

But the very mention of shipbuilding in the Chronicle seems to have been enough to initiate an inviolable tradition. In the millenary year, 1901, the Royal Navy launched an armoured cruiser named *King Alfred*. The picture that illustrated the invitation to the launch of the new ship reinforces the sense that myth was more inspiring than historical precedent. In it a version of one of Alfred's ships is imagined alongside the cruiser. As one historian has remarked, it 'appears to have been modelled on Noah's ark'. In 1922 Colin Gill revisited the maritime theme in another decoration for the Palace of Westminster, where the Vikings' running aground at Swanage in 877 after a 'great storm at sea' (when the Chronicle tells us they lost 120 ships) becomes another famous naval victory for Alfred's longships.

The naval connection is also illustrative of the way that

Alfred's reputation could be put to use beyond England. In the United States interest in the Anglo-Saxons ran high from independence. Jefferson, a keen Anglo-Saxonist (though more often thought of as a classicist), suggested that the Great Seal of the United States should carry images of Hengist and Horsa, traditionally the first Anglo-Saxon kings, 'from whom we claim the honor of being descended, and whose political principles and form of government we have assumed'. This idea fitted well with Jefferson's more general cleaving to Anglo-Saxon precedent and his desire for what he called a 'restitution of the ancient Saxon laws'. Although the seal suggestion didn't bear fruit, an earlier connection had already been made. When the Continental Navy was initiated during the American Revolution, one of the first ships, originally the *Black Prince*, was renamed *Alfred* in December 1775; it became the American flagship, commanded by the fleet's most famous captain, John Paul Jones, and engaged on several occasions with the Royal Navy, after whose 'founder' it was named. The figurehead of a warrior holding a sword was unchanged, but did as well for King Alfred as for the son of Edward III.

To the American Revolutionaries, fighting against monarchical tyranny embodied by George III, King Alfred was paradoxically a symbol of liberty. The connection would continue to be appealed to, with a significant American contingent involved in the Winchester millenary, for example, and affiliated events, included a 'banquet at Delmonico's', New York, on the other side of the Atlantic. At Winchester, US General Rockwell assured his audience that 'Alfred the Great is a household word on the other side of the Atlantic, quite as much as here in England, for he was our king just as much as he was yours': the embodiment of Anglo-Saxon qualities of 'self-reliance and individual freedom'. This Alfred is a far cry from the ninth-century king who, while saving his people from the oppression of a foreign occupier, most probably restricted rather than expanded his subjects' freedoms. The exigencies of what has become known in our age as 'homeland security' made the same demand in Alfred's time as they do in ours: an expectation from those protected that they accept what we have seen one historian calling 'new and burdensome institutions' (in Chapter 5). The burghal system, the reorganised military obligations, even Alfred's educational reforms, all restricted rather than expanded his people's everyday liberty, though of course Alfred would have argued that they saved them too.

Alfred as a symbol of freedom was, however, an inheritance from the old country, not an American invention. The transformation into the ideal of the 'founder of English liberty' (as the inscription on the eighteenth-century folly at Stourhead, Wiltshire, known as King Alfred's Tower has it) seems to have begun in earnest in the sixteenth and seventeenth centuries. Alfred's reputation began to be contested between different sides of political opinion, using it as a model for constitutional monarchy, guaranteeing ancient freedoms, on the one hand, or a paragon of unquestionable royal authority on the other. Although Alfred's semi-mythical establishment of a monarchy under the law had been celebrated in the thirteenth-century *Mirror of Justices* attributed to the fishmonger-turned-legal historian Andrew Horn, it was not until the Civil War year of 1642 that a printed version of that work appeared, with three more editions before the Restoration and subsequent translations from the French emerging sporadically up to 1840 (and a critical edition in 1893). The seventeenth-century publication followed on from a more recent tradition, begun by Archbishop Parker, that saw Alfred as the 'first monarch'. By the time of the reign of Charles I the king could be employed as propaganda pin-up by both sides of the political debate. The first post-Asser Life of Alfred, by Robert Powell, in 1634, was a royalist tract presented as a parallel biography that specifically compared the two monarchs as a 'paire of Peerlesse Princes'. Sir John Spelman's *Life of Alfred* (1643) was dedicated to the prince of Wales, the future Charles II, and saw Alfred as the 'First Founder of the English monarchy'.

On the parliamentarian side Alfred was also put to work. In Milton's *Eikonoklastes* (1649) there is a discussion of 'Alfred, the most worthy king['s]' coronation oath, which (conveniently) made the king subject to the law. Needless to say, no genuine record of Alfred's coronation oath survived then or is known to us now. Milton's citation, along with another that attributes biennial parliaments to Anglo-Saxon precedent, comes originally from Horn's *Mirror of Justices*, to which can be attributed much of the spurious 'authority' that the association of Alfred with constitutional monarchy gained from the seventeenth century onwards. Alfred became part of the 'Norman Yoke' theory of English history, in which he was seen as a guardian of the ancient liberties on which William the Conqueror, and his successors up to Charles I, were deemed to have trampled. Alfred is essential to any notion of continuity in this argument, as the ideal of a just Anglo-Saxon king. In the seventeenth and eighteenth centuries it was important to establish long historical precedent for now abused rights, as in Nathaniel Bacon's *Historical Discourse of the Uniformity of the Government of England* (1647), rather than to be seen arguing for something new. In these terms Alfred could be as well employed to represent the limiting ideal of a founding constitutional monarch as to legitimate the actions and claims of later monarchs. But it is to Horn and his followers, rather than the historical Alfred, that we should attribute this view.

Later political uses of Alfred in the late seventeenth and eighteenth century would continue to emphasise him as a constitutional rather than an absolute monarch. Alfred became the historical champion of the 'country-party', the 'patriot opposition' to the government of Robert Walpole that saw his regime as usurping the rights of the king-in-parliament. A relatively newly established 'county family' such as the Hoares, at Stourhead, formerly the seat of Lord Stourton, could connect themselves both to the locality's distant past and to traditions kept alive in the present by invoking Alfred. It is in this context that we should place the building of King Alfred's Tower (1772) – on the supposed site of Egbert's Stone, mustering place before Edington – at Stourhead, with its maximalist view of Alfred's founding achievements:

Alfred the Great ...
On this summit erected his
standard against Danish
invaders. To him we owe the
origin of Juries, the establishment
of a Militia, the creation of a
Naval Force.
Alfred, the light of a
benighted age was a
philosopher and a Christian,
the father of his people,
the founder of the English
MONARCHY and of LIBERTY

23. *A drawing of King Alfred's Tower, an eighteenth-century folly by Henry Flitcroft, which memorialises Alfred as the font of post-Glorious Revolutionary freedoms.*

EMPIRE AND ENGLAND

The restoration of the monarchy, and the limiting of its powers after the Glorious Revolution of 1688, did not extinguish Alfred's symbolic history. He continued to be used as a malleable representative of different party lines, though the more successful protests could be amalgamated into establishment thinking as their original context faded. Although James Thomson and David Mallet's *Alfred: A Masque* (1740) was first written and performed for Frederick, prince of Wales, the son of George II and the focus of opposition to Walpole, its lasting success, outliving the unfortunate

Frederick, meant that Alfred became assimilated with both the ruling royal line (especially when it experienced injections of Germanic blood) and the imperial assumptions of Britain. 'Rule Britannia', the closing chorus of Thomson and Mallett's masque, specifically casts Alfred as the progenitor not just of England or Britain but of the British empire. That chorus would, of course, in turn become completely divorced from its origins. By the time it became the subject of arguments surrounding the programme for the Last Night of the Proms in 2001, which came shortly after the terrorist attacks on the USA of September 11, 'Rule Britannia' was objected to as an outdated and embarrassing imperialist aria, and Alfred's name, a source of transatlantic mutual pride exactly a century earlier, was never mentioned.

In the nineteenth century the association of Alfred and empire took root, with references to imperial greatness scattered throughout the millenary celebrations at Winchester, for example. Typical was *The Times*'s leading article on the millenary, describing Alfred's Winchester as the 'earliest organic germ of the British Empire of our own day'. A gift in this respect was the Chronicle's reference to alms going from Alfred's court to India in 883, though it is likely that the reference is actually to 'Judea'.

It is easy to put the associations of Alfred and empire to one side, as a clear case of later manipulation of the name of a king who had no ambitions or capabilities beyond his own shores. But Alfred as the unifier of England is a notion with a much stronger hold, despite the fact that it too relies on projecting later developments back on to the ninth century. To begin with, without the impact of the Vikings there seems little reason to expect that England should begin to graduate towards unification at a time around Alfred's reign. Some of the smaller kingdoms – of Deira, Kent, Sussex, the Hwicce, Lindsey and Essex – had already been assimilated into the four larger ones – Northumbria, Wessex, Mercia and East Anglia – but there is no justification for viewing England's unification around this time as inevitable if the Vikings are taken out of the equation. By removing the established royal lines of the other English kingdoms the Viking invasions created the environment for this fundamental shift in English politics. But even so, it is difficult to argue that Alfred even had a consistent vision of a unified England, let alone went any way to achieving it.

The idea of an authority beyond the four kingdoms had existed before Alfred's time. The Anglo-Saxons had arrived in the Roman province of Britannia, so the concept of Britain, or at least England, under a single ruler did not have to be invented. Famously, Bede, writing in the early eighth century, has a list of seven kings whose 'imperium' extended beyond their kingdoms, and the list is added to by a Chronicle entry for the year 825. That entry also gives us the term *bryten-walda* or *bretwalda* (depending on the manuscript consulted), meaning 'mighty ruler' or 'ruler of Britain'. Historians have long debated the practical meaning of this title. Some powerful kings who dominated their neighbours, such as Offa of Mercia, did not apparently receive it. In fact, after Alfred's grandfather Egbert is accorded it by the Chronicle (begun, of course, in Alfred's own time), it does not appear again. But perhaps the important notion to grasp is one that saw authority as extending more over people than over territory. In most charters, for example, kings describe themselves as 'of the Mercians', 'of the people of Kent', or 'of the West Saxons', rather than of the kingdom itself. Before Alfred's time, while Christian lords of areas outside Wessex existed,

24. *The only coin of Alfred where he is described as 'Rex-Anglo'.*

there could be no prospect of a permanent extension of authority. Once the Vikings had removed them, the natural order of things, as Alfred's writing and lawmaking suggest, would imply that another Christian lord would eventually fill the vacuum. And Bede, the originator of ideas of a united English identity, may have formed part of Alfred's translation programme, though it was not one of the works the king translated himself.

Alfred's own titles did extend beyond king of the West Saxons, though it may be wishful thinking of Asser to address him as king 'Anglorum Saxonum' – of the Anglo-Saxons – as well as ruler of all the Christians of Great Britain. He appears in charters as 'King of the English', and a single coin has been found with the style 'Rex Anglo'. In 886, after Alfred formally took London from the Vikings, the Chronicle tells us that 'all the English people that were not under subjection to the Danes submitted to him'. But the key phrase is 'not under subjection to the Danes'. While the Viking occupation lasted, as it did well beyond Alfred's reign, the idea of a unified Anglo-Saxon England was only that. It is more significant in this context that Alfred entrusted London to his Mercian son-in-law Aethelred, who remained in charge until well after Alfred's death. Only when Aethelred died, in 910 or 911, did Alfred's successor, Edward the Elder, succeed to 'London and Oxford and all the lands' in the possession of Aethelred and his wife. In fact, the Chronicle's West Saxon bias is evident even in that statement, as Aethelred's widow, Edward's sister Aethelflaed, continued a vigorous campaign of reclaiming Mercia from Viking encroachment until her death in 918; only then, when Edward prevented her daughter from succeeding, can Mercia truly be said to have fallen under West Saxon rule. Alfred's reign and his ambitions may be seen as part of the unifying story, but they neither began it nor ended it. To call Alfred the unifier of England is of a piece with calling him the Father of the Navy. The crucial periods for both developments came either earlier, in terms of the origination of the idea, or much later, in terms of making the idea a recognisable reality.

As far as a unified England is concerned, Alfred's role was more to sustain and give momentum to long-standing concepts than to initiate or fully to realise them. It was his son and daughter, Edward the Elder and Aethelflaed, who began to expand West Saxon rule into Viking Mercia, and his grandson Aethelstan who took Northumbria in 927, becoming the first true king of England. There were some set-backs even then, until 959, and the succession of Edgar 'the peaceable'. Aethelstan and Edgar later dropped out of the popular account. Elsewhere the power of stories has been seen to lie behind the fixing of certain versions of Alfred's image. But no story illustrates Alfred as founder of England. From very early on, however, historians projected what to them seemed the quintessential achievement of any Anglo-Saxon king on to the most famous. In the twelfth century the monastic historian Orderic Vitalis described Alfred as the 'first king to hold sway over the whole of England', and such formulations stuck. The wisps of evidence that misleadingly supported this assumption kept it alive because Alfred's reputation, so often backed up by memorable stories, looms so convincingly large in other areas. Without a similar armoury of contemporary witness and popular tradition Aethelstan and Edgar's more verifiable claims have faded from popular view.

Perhaps the explanation for Alfred's receiving popular credit also has something to do with the impression he leaves of being the founder, if not of England, then of English. His decision to promote the reading and writing of the language that, however distantly, is connected to the one we speak today is, of course, a far more lasting legacy than the mere assimilation of territory. And if Alfred's educational and literary policies had specific religious and political dimensions that tied them very firmly to his time and his circumstances, nevertheless he seems to stand at the beginning of something significant. There had been translations into Old English before Alfred – the Venerable Bede had translated parts of the Bible, for example – but the Vikings enforced a definitive break with the literary past. The high point of Old English literary excellence may have come after Alfred, for instance with the homilies of Aelfric at the end of the tenth century. But Alfred's revival and the manner of it, making it a central part of a political programme, were unique. The political obsessions of the seventeenth and eighteenth centuries may have obscured this significance, but with the rise of Old English literary scholarship in the nineteenth and twentieth centuries the importance of Alfred and English, as against Alfred and England, began to be established.

Recently historians have begun to connect Alfred's literary programme to a more general seeking out of a new English identity, coalescing around the word *Angelcynn*, used for instance in his Preface to the *Pastoral Care*, to mean England. Though that noun is known first to scholars in a Mercian context in the 850s, it is under Alfred that it crops up more frequently. What is particularly notable about this usage is that, simply put, Alfred's own people were not Angles of any description, but Saxons. In choosing to use the word *Angelcynn*, Alfred seems to have been making a specific effort to reach out to Christians beyond Wessex's borders. None of this means that Alfred had a vision of united England in mind, but it may persuade us that, with Bede, he saw the potential of a common identity and wished to name it.

Alfred's legal code, which included reference to Mercian precedent, may have formed part of this promotion of a new sense of common identity. But when later observers looked back on Alfred's reign, as Henry Hoare did at Stourhead, they exacerbated a long-standing tendency to ascribe things they approved of to Anglo-Saxon England by attributing as many of them as possible to its most famous king. Thus, inevitably, Alfred is described in the Stourhead inscription as the king to whom 'we owe the origin of juries'. In the chapter of this book that discussed Alfred and the law juries were not mentioned. That is because there is no evidence, nor even any lasting anecdotal tradition, that they existed in Alfred's time. The historical discussion over the origins of the jury is vast and complex, but the earliest mention in an Anglo-Saxon context of something even like a jury is in a late tenth-century law code of Aethelred II, where 'the twelve leading thegns' of specific districts are enjoined to 'accuse no innocent man nor conceal any guilty one'. The idea that Alfred had anything to do with juries seems again to begin with Horn's *Mirror of Justices*. It was perpetuated by one of Alfred's seventeenth-century biographers, Sir John Spelman. Unlike the attribution of a unified England or the paternity of the Royal Navy, the idea that Alfred initiated the jury has not lasted. It fell to a series of technical assaults by nineteenth- and twentieth-century legal and constitutional historians, of whom the most famous, F. W. Maitland, seemed to take great delight in squashing any romantic fantasies about Anglo-Saxon twelve good men and true. 'This "palladium of our liberties"', he wrote, 'is in its origin not English but Frankish.'

The enthusiasm for discovering Alfredian origins could lead the most respectable institutions astray. The association of Alfred with a united England or with juries is the result of exaggerating the historical record. But exaggeration would be too kind a description of the way that Alfred was linked with the foundation of the University of Oxford, the result of a brazen embellishment of a medieval story that led Maitland to describe 'lying' as the 'earliest form of inter-university sports'. The seventeenth-century antiquary William Camden seems to have been the victim of an academic spoof when his assistants included a bogus account of Alfred's foundation of Oxford University in Camden's collection of historical documents, published in 1602. The claim was eagerly taken up by the university, with busts and statues commissioned, and was even confirmed in an eighteenth-century court action. The Oxford association is the reason why the most famous archaeological finding connected to Alfred's reign, the Alfred Jewel, was given to the

25. *The Prince and Princess of Wales arrive to unveil Count Gleichen's statue at Wantage, 1877. Though thousands had turned out in 1849 to celebrate the millenary of Alfred's birth there, a public subscription for a statue in his name had not attracted much support, and it wasn't until a benefactor, Robert Loyd-Lindsay, later Lord Wantage, put up the money that a statue could be commissioned.*

university's Ashmolean Museum. It has been pointed out that the mania for having Alfred as the university's founder has rather obscured the far more likely possibility (disputed, but for which there is some archaeological evidence) that he established the town of Oxford.

Wantage, Alfred's birthplace, had mixed fortunes in its attempts to claim its most famous son. But, another urban association, with Winchester, was embraced with more durable results than either Oxford or Wantage achieved. Winchester is often described as Alfred's 'capital', but there is no real evidence that it was. Asser doesn't mention

Winchester, and the Chronicle places Alfred there only once, when he had some Viking prisoners hanged in the town in 896. Though he was buried there, his grave was lost, and it was only in histories of the town written from the fifteenth century onwards that a Winchester legend began to grow for Alfred. The culmination, of course, was the millenary celebrations and Hamo Thornycroft's statue, unveiled in 1901. Without the energy of the Winchester mayor at the millenary, Alfred Bowker, it is likely that the Alfredian connection would be confined to local legend. Bowker was in no doubt that he wanted the celebrations, and the statue, to make a national (and international) impact. The size of the millenary events, only slightly scaled down when the deaths of Queen Victoria and the assassinated US President McKinley occurred as the ceremonies were being prepared, matched the ambitions of Bowker for the statue. Thornycroft records a conversation with the mayor in which Bowker explained his idea: 'We want a big statue, one which folk can see as they fly by in the express.' Thornycroft's response that 'Since one can hardly see the Cathedral under those conditions, you must not expect me to make a statue bigger than that!' only slightly dimmed Bowker's ardour: 'Well then, make it as big as you can.' The colossal result may not be visible from the express, but it has ensured that Alfred will be associated with Winchester for as long as it stands, however tenuous the king's historical connections with the city.

The steady discrediting of most of Alfred's 'founding' achievements may seem to have left him in some ways a reduced figure. More rigorous scholarship has shown the majority of these associations to be exaggerations or inventions of later ages. Alfred did found things, including towns and abbeys, and he initiated things, such as the Anglo-Saxon

Chronicle. But he is more convincing as an agent of continuity. This was, after all, how he saw himself – not as a founder but a restorer, not as a forger of new paths but, as he puts it in the Preface to the *Pastoral Care*, a seeker after others' tracks. Innovation, whether in military or naval arts, in government or in scholarship, was always tempered with tradition. However adaptable Alfred's legend proved, he was overwhelmingly a man of his own time.

10

DYING TO BE FAMOUS: ALFRED'S POSTHUMOUS RISE AND FALL

After his death in 899, what historians have christened the 'cult of Alfred' did not spring up immediately. This would come as no surprise to anyone who merely read the entries in the Anglo-Saxon Chronicle for the years around his demise. They tell us simply that Alfred died, that he was 'king over the whole English people except for that part which was under Danish rule' and the number of years he reigned. The Chronicle doesn't even mention where he was buried, as it does for his predecessors Aethelbald (in Sherborne) and Aethelred (in Wimborne Minster). Asser, of course, wrote his biography during Alfred's lifetime and apparently did not return to it after 893, the year in which it was probably composed, so, although his book would become the cornerstone of Alfred's legend in later years, at the moment of his death he can give no obituary or even help locate Alfred's grave. Only the late tenth-century chronicle of Ealdorman Aethelweard, based on a lost version of the Anglo-Saxon Chronicle but with the writer's own additions, tells us that Alfred was buried at Winchester and gives him a more ringing send-off: to Aethelweard, Alfred was the 'magnanimous ... king of the Saxons, unshakeable pillar of the western people, a man replete with justice, vigorous in warfare, learned in speech, above all instructed in divine learning'.

Aethelweard was writing at a time when Alfred's line had established its authority over the whole of England but was once again threatened by Viking attackers. So Alfred, who had successfully resisted the Vikings from a much weaker position, would have seemed a good role model. This set a pattern for Alfred's posthumous 'employment'. In later centuries, as we have seen, Alfred was invoked as the founder of everything from the Royal Navy to the British Empire. At the time of his death, however, the Chronicle is far more concerned with contemporary politics. What the entry for his death year makes clear is that even the succession of Alfred's own son to the throne was not exactly secure. Edward had to deal with a full-scale rebellion led by his cousin Aethelwold, the son of Alfred's older brother Aethelred (from whom Alfred had inherited), who might well have had legitimate expectations of succession. Alfred had done his best to give his son the advantage in any anticipated struggle, granting him a large portion of personal land in his will, designating him his successor and trying to mollify Aethelwold and his brother without giving them much of a power base. But this could only weigh the odds in his son's favour, not guarantee his smooth succession.

At first Aethelwold resisted with his own force, but after evading Edward's army he joined up with the Vikings of Northumbria, who, according to most versions of the Chronicle (though not, significantly, the version most strongly associated with Wessex), 'accepted him as king and gave allegiance to him'. This was a serious challenge, which rapidly turned into a full-scale invasion; Aethelwold secured the help of the East Anglian Vikings as well and in 902 fought a pitched battle with Edward's forces. Aethelwold was killed in that battle, but it was not until four years later, in 906, that Edward 'established' peace with the Northumbrians and East Angles. Clearly in its early stages Edward's inheritance was anything but straightforward. His opponent's willingness to form an alliance with the 'heathen' Vikings also puts into context the construction of them as the natural enemy of the Anglo-Saxons. As we have seen, in Alfred's time resistance to the Vikings was a matter of life and death, and a religious imperative. But in an internecine power struggle they became legitimate players in the game.

It is impossible to know whether, had he succeeded in his bid for the crown, Aethelwold would have become a client king, like the men the Vikings installed in Northumbria and Mercia, Egbert and Ceolwulf. Certainly, the steady 'reconquest' of Viking Mercia and Northumbria that took place under Edward and his successors would have been unlikely if his cousin had triumphed. When we talk of the legacy of Alfred, of him as founder of a line that united England, it is important to see how fragile that legacy was in its early stages. The Chronicle's relatively terse entry reflects that, and shows that to describe its approach as Alfredian 'propaganda' can be an exaggeration. The entries for the earlier years of Alfred's reign, as those for the years before it, had all been written retrospectively; but in this period, when the entries were probably being written much more closely to the events they describe, the chance to editorialise was much smaller. It also seems as though no one troubled to doctor what had been written at a later stage. The annals reflect a West Saxon royal view, but they do not concentrate their favours on Alfred, instead viewing the current king as the most important.

After death, as in life, then, Alfred's prospects were uncertain at first. Alive, Alfred had had to overcome the unlikelihood of a youngest son succeeding to the throne and then to reclaim his kingdom when all seemed lost. But the seriousness of Aethelwold's threat to Edward's succession shows that Alfred's hard work, often described as 'laying the foundations' for the building of the English monarchy by his successors, was no guarantee of that outcome. If Aethelwold's bid had worked, Alfred would be barely remembered; even if Aethelwold's Viking allies had allowed him a measure of independence, we can be sure he would have written Alfred out of the record, and Asser's book, as well as the popular anecdotal tradition that it can be seen as engendering, might well have been suppressed.

Edward's defeat of his cousin preserved Alfred's name. In the previous chapter we saw how Alfred's reputation as an English 'founding father' was constructed on more or less imaginary grounds in the centuries following his death. These were the ingredients of Alfred's public, political and 'official' legacy, but he gradually also became the focus of a more informal, poetic and mythical set of ideas, which contributed just as much to his reputation over time. Alfred's uniqueness as a posthumous 'invention' lies in the combination of the personal and the political, the individual as well as the king, in his legend. Alfred's personal myth hovered and settled on various different themes over the centuries. We have seen throughout this book how much stories contributed to the way in which different episodes from Alfred's life have been viewed. The growing-up of a mythical Alfred is often related to these stories but at times seems to take on a life of its own.

The conventional way in which a personal cult of a medieval or early medieval king began was around his body. The remains of Alfred's contemporary St Edmund, for example, were moved at some point in the tenth century from the place of his martyrdom at the hands of the Vikings to the abbey at Bury, and there became the object of pilgrimage and veneration up to the dissolution of the monasteries. Alfred's body did not inspire similar piety, though it too was moved to a new resting place, in his son Edward the Elder's New Minster at Winchester. Although the thief Helmstan, as we saw in Chapter 6, used Alfred's tomb as a way of getting protection from the law, there is no record of a more general pilgrimage to his burial place. On the contrary, William of Malmesbury, whose twelfth-century account of Alfred's life is one of the fullest and most laudatory after Asser's, has a story explaining the translation of Alfred's remains not as an act of filial honour but as the solution to a supernatural problem. The 'deluded canons' of Alfred's initial burial place, William writes, 'maintained that the king's ghost returned to his dead body and wandered at night through their lodgings, and so his son and successor took up his father's remains and laid them in peace in a new monastery'. So Alfred's first, inauspicious manifestation as a figure of posthumous influence is as an unwelcome ghost.

In fact, while Alfred's reputation was almost exclusively in the hands of monks and churchmen, it was not necessarily secure. A king who has rarely received much 'revisionist' treatment from historians, even in our more sceptical age, was admonished during his own reign, if a letter from Pope John VIII to Aethelred, archbishop of Canterbury, in 877/8, is to be believed, 'not to be disobedient' to the Church. The pope advised the archbishop, at the height of the Viking invasions, to 'resist strenuously' not the invaders but his own king. We do not know why the archbishop was complaining, and unsurprisingly neither Asser nor the Chronicle tells us, but the judgement of a twelfth-century Abingdon monastic chronicler, that Alfred was a 'Judas' who had snatched the institution's land, suggests that Alfred may have been trying to turn the Vikings' depredations to his advantage by claiming as royal land that the Church believed was its own.

What we might see as the sharp practice of a canny political operator could have seriously affected Alfred's chances of becoming a popular hero, if such stories had caught on. But in 1,100 years this, and the tales of the king's early 'licentiousness' from which his piety saved him, are all the blemishes that Alfred has suffered. This is the man whom David Hume 'wished to see ... delineated in more lively colours, and with more particular strokes, that we may at least perceive some of those small specks and blemishes, from which, as a man, it is impossible he could be entirely exempted'. That is, Hume assumed he wasn't perfect; he just didn't have any authority for saying so. Despite clerical objections and the apparent lack of a cult around his tomb, Alfred's piety was more generally thought so unimpeachable that he came within a whisker of following the more conventional medieval route to popularity, by becoming a saint. In 1441 Henry VI put Alfred's name forward to the pope for canonisation. He was turned down. (Could papal memory have been long enough to recall how a predecessor had once viewed the king as an enemy of the church?) Another name put forward at the same time was accepted: Osmund of Salisbury, whose subsequent fame suggests that sainthood is no guarantee of remembrance. After the Reformation the Anglican Church, which doesn't canonise, did grant Alfred a feast day, though this wasn't formalised until the twentieth century (when

26 October, the day of his death in 899, was made Alfred's 'black letter day').

Though 'goodness' would underwrite his posthumous fame as much as 'greatness', Alfred's journey into the popular imagination would take a slightly less conventional route than the martyr's way. From his own time and throughout the Middle Ages Alfred's reputation as a remarkable man almost outran his deeds as a king. This process began, of course, with Asser, who established the qualities for which Alfred has been commended ever since. The two that captured subsequent writers' imagination were his wisdom and his honesty. Asser calls Alfred *veredicus*, truth-teller, a description repeated by the Annals of St Neots, one of the sources for the story of the cakes. The idea of a king who told the truth was so remarkable that it stuck fast. A thousand years later Lord Rosebery's millenary speech was on the subject of 'Alfred the truth-teller'; perhaps the former prime minister hoped that some of the West Saxon reputation for probity would rub off on him.

Two works of the mid-twelfth or early thirteenth century attest to Alfred's growing reputation for wisdom. Where Asser had specifically portrayed his master as a latter-day Solomon (see Chapter 7), these later medieval versions of the king had him as a more practical wise man. The first collection, known as *The Proverbs of Alfred*, is dated to a time around the anarchy of Stephen's reign (1135–54). It tells of an assembly at Seaford in Sussex when Alfred, 'the protector and darling of the English', advised his listeners 'how they were to lead their lives'. This is the king as agony aunt, pronouncing on self-reliance, the virtues of hard work, the temporary nature of wealth, mortality, parenting, alcohol, matrimony, friendship, women, gossip, honesty, old age and death. In the long anonymous poem *The Owl and the Nightingale*, generally dated to the reign of Henry II, which followed Stephen's (though the surviving manuscripts are later), Alfred is a less forbidding source of authority, invoked nine times in the debate between the two birds. The wisdom on display here ranges from matters of politics – 'If you see a threat before it has arrived, it will lose almost all its strength' – to ones of personal hygiene – 'Someone who knows he's fouled himself keeps out of the way.'

ALFRED AND ARTHUR

At around the same time as these works were renewing Alfred's legend as the wise king, another royal figure was being 'discovered', whose myth would eventually over-shadow Alfred's: King Arthur. Geoffrey of Monmouth's *History of the Kings of Britain*, completed in 1139, was almost single-handedly responsible for introducing the legendary Celtic king to later readers. Subsequent works by Wace and Layamon (the first English treatment) would elaborate the story. But Alfred's reputation as 'England's Darling', a for-mulation used of him by the thirteenth-century Layamon in his Old English Arthurian epic *Brut* as well as the earlier *Proverbs*, should not necessarily be seen as vying with that of the chief subject of Layamon's poem. The remarkable thing about the mythical Alfred is that he was a well-attested his-torical figure to whom stories and beliefs became attached. By contrast, though there may well have been a historical Arthur, around the sixth century AD, there are no contem-porary records of him, and even a hundred years later he is barely mentioned in accounts of 'his' time. Before Geoffrey of Monmouth discovered 'a very ancient book in the British tongue' – almost certainly a fabrication – upon which his version of the Arthurian legend is 'based', Arthur was unknown. Arthur is almost all myth, with a grain of history. Alfred's posthumous make-up is the opposite.

As with Alfred, Arthur's fortunes depended in part on contemporary politics. Preoccupation with Arthurian themes took off in the twelfth century, when, as well as a literary revival, the location of Arthur's tomb was thought to have been discovered. Richard I even took a sword named Excalibur on crusade with him, though he gave it away. Elaborations of Arthur's story continued to appear throughout the Middle Ages, giving poetic fuel to the age of chivalry. Malory's *Morte d'Arthur* in 1471 was the most lavish and detailed version of the legends, though the circumstances in which it was written – its author imprisoned, possibly on charges of rape, assault and theft – make a telling contrast with the ideals it represented. Only fourteen years later the accession of Henry Tudor, with his Welsh, 'Celtic' antecedents, also gave impetus to the idea of Arthur as the quintessential 'British' king (Henry's eldest son was named Arthur, though he predeceased his brother Henry VIII). It was not all one-way traffic: in the eighteenth century a combination of political and antiquarian inspiration seems to have caused Lord Bathurst to change the name of his 'King Arthur's Castle' to 'Alfred's Hall'. But it was not until Alfred's brief moment of blanket coverage in the excitement surrounding his millennial year that Arthur was ever (briefly) eclipsed in popularity.

By the twentieth century the two kings were so regularly mixed up – Alfred having become as distant and historically unfamiliar a character as his legendary predecessor – that some could make a joke of it. In *1066 and All That* Sellar and

Yeatman caution that 'Alfred ought never to be confused with King Arthur, equally memorable, but probably non-existent and therefore perhaps less important historically (unless he did exist).' They go on to refer to 'King Arthur and the cakes', his 'marine inventions', and 'Arthur, Lord Tennyson's' famous line 'Then slowly answered Alfred from the marsh'. If my own experiences in the course of writing this book are at all typical, the confusion has only deepened since. I have lost count of the number of times that helpful friends have pointed out articles, books, films and television programmes that 'could be useful': all of them about King Arthur.

The Arthurian comparison demonstrates the limits of Alfred's legend. For all the stories and mythical accretion to his name Alfred has rarely entered the popular consciousness to the same extent. At the time of the millenary a *Punch* cartoon could play on an apparently universal sharing in Alfred mania. But when Hamo Thornycroft was at work in his studio on his Alfred statue, an electrician asked him who it was he was sculpting. The answer obviously didn't mean much to him, in Thornycroft's recollection: '"King Alfred what?" said he. "Alfred the Great." "Well, he's a big 'un. He's got a good-sized foot."'

A FASHIONABLE KING

If the trail left in popular culture by Alfred is less spectacular than Arthur's, it is substantial enough. The real beginning of the more 'official' if just as a-historical Alfredian myth can probably be located to Andrew Horn's *Mirror of Justices*, which began the practice of associating Alfred with institutions of which the writer approved. From there, as we have

HISTORY REPEATS ITSELF
Mistress: 'How is this Mary? Reading – and the cakes burning in the oven!'
Mary: 'Very sorry, Mum; but I was so interested in King Alfred's Millinery!'

26. From Punch, *18 September 1901, when Alfred mania was deemed to afflict all classes.*

seen, the exercise of connecting Alfred to the writer's cause took any number of forms. The preservation of popular traditions is likely to have been less secure, especially if Alfred became, as seems likely, the focus of an oral tradition. So it is not surprising that the popular trail of Alfred's reputation goes cold for a long time, even while his more 'official'

27. *Woodcuts illustrating a seventeenth-century ballad about Alfred, which includes what a nineteenth-century editor's introduction describes as 'an equal combat of four hours' duration between the Shepherd and King Alfred in disguise', though the concealment has not run to removing his crown.*

incarnation was beginning to take shape. The first popular manifestation of Alfred after the wisdom literature of the Middle Ages was in a ballad, 'The Shepherd and the King, and of Gillian, the Shepherd's Wife, and her Churlish Answers: Being Full of Mirth and Merry Past Time', known at its earliest in 1578. That is four years after Archbishop Parker's first printed edition of Asser's Life, including the story of the cakes. We cannot know if Parker's Asser revived or (surely less likely) inspired the ballad, but it recounts Alfred's lowest ebb around Athelney, and the story of the cakes, in breezy style. Rather than being forced into hiding, Alfred decides to slum it with his people: 'liking well' their 'Churlish glee', he 'forsoke his stately Court: / And in disguise unknowne went forth, / to see that joviall sport'. The Chronicle and Asser's fugitive king 'in great distress' is replaced by a merry monarch 'coasting through Somerset shire'. Three woodcuts illustrate the first printing of the ballad, showing the king being taken in by the shepherd and beaten with a stick by his wife when he burns the cakes. Perhaps the artist wasn't confident that his readers would recognize the king, as in spite of the ballad's description of his disguise including swapping his 'crowne' for 'a Monmouth cap', Alfred is shown in full regalia throughout.

In the seventeenth century Alfred's historical reputation began its long revival in earnest, and he was the object of study for antiquarians and biographers, William Camden, Robert Powell and Sir John Spelman among them. Though their work provided inspiration for one seventeenth-century Alfred play, William Drury's Latin *Alvredus*, it was in the following century, as more historians began to write about and praise Alfred, that his story was more frequently dramatised. From the eighteenth century onwards, though writers and artists would continue to take extreme liberties with what they understood of the historical record, their interpretations could be traced, however faintly, to the work of historians. So the popular and the 'institutional' Alfred began to combine in artistic renditions.

This new authority was no guarantee of lasting success, however. The only dramatic interpretation that has lasted at all is Thomson and Mallet's *Alfred: A Masque*, which, thanks to Arne's music, still receives the very occasional revival in full (and can be found as a recording), as well as its closing chorus's annual outing in London's Albert Hall. Around the time of the masque's greatest popularity, however, Alfred's fame was by no means confined to British jingoists. The source for many of the dramatic and poetic reconstructions of the eighteenth century was a French work, Paul de Rapin-Thoyras's *Histoire d'Angleterre* (1724), in which the author declared it a 'shame' that the English nation was 'now so ignorant, having had a king so wise'. In the same century, he would be apotheosised by Voltaire, Mirabeau and Herder, among others. Both Haydn and Donizetti composed on an Alfredian theme. In the next century the German historian Reinhold Pauli's biography was written in reaction to the revolutionary events in his homeland of 1848. As Thomas Hughes approvingly put it, in his 1869 improving work on Alfred, Pauli's book was 'written by a German for Germans'.

Most English dramatic interpretations of Alfred, however, have left as little mark on the popular consciousness as John Home's *Alfred: A Tragedy* (1777), which, the playwright admitted, 'signally failed'. At least Home's tragedy was produced, at the Theatre Royal in Convent Garden. Alexander Bicknell's *The Patriot King: or Alfred and Elvida, an Historical Tragedy* (1788) 'failed to find a stage'. Nor can one say that the failure was because these and other treatments made Alfred's story a tragic one. Only in scholarly articles and books will you find reference to an Alfred ballet, featuring Grimaldi the clown, or a *Harlequin Alfred the Great!, or, The Magic Banjo, and the Mystic Raven!*, of 1850, though that production's inclusion of Alfred blacking up as an Ethiopian minstrel to gain entry to Guthrum's camp would have accounted for its demise in our own time.

It was already remarked in 1841 that Alfred 'has had the fortune to be treated only by writers of subordinate powers'. Where Arthur had Malory and Tennyson, Alfred had names that have for the most part been justly forgotten. In the nineteenth century what Alfredian poetry lacked in quality it certainly made up for in quantity. Sir Richard Blackmore's 1723 *Alfred, An Epick Poem* – dedicated, like Thomson and Mallet's masque, to Prince Frederick – seemed already to have set a record at twelve books, and the poet was forced to send the Anglo-Saxon king on a Mediterranean cruise as far as Tunis to fill his pages. But the new century began with Joseph Cottle's twenty-four book epic *Alfred*, which a modern scholar has charitably described as the 'least unsuccessful' of the 'longer poems on Alfred'. Though one poet laureate, Alfred Austin, would take the *Proverbs* as partial inspiration for his verse drama *England's Darling* (1896), a predecessor in the post, Henry James Pye, took up the long-distance challenge laid down by Blackmore and Cottle by producing his epic Alfred in 1815. But John Fitchett, between 1808 and his death thirty years later, outdid them all, spawning a monster that extended over forty-seven books, 'estimated' at 130,000 lines: it may be the longest poem ever written in English. It has also been described, as far as the not very distinguished category of Alfred poetry goes, as the 'worst'.

Some good poets wrote on Alfred, including Wordsworth, though his two short works on the king are not among his best. Wordsworth's 'Ecclesiastical Sonnet XXVI' crams in reference to the king's piety, his military success and his musicianship and is Hume-like in its brooking no equal to the king. Chesterton's *Ballad of the White Horse* seems more successful, if only because it faces up to the difficulty of presenting a historical figure mythically, confessing freely in a preface that 'all of it that is not frankly fictitious, as in any prose romance about the past, is meant to emphasize tradition rather than history'. But by the time Chesterton wrote (in 1911), it was more common for Alfredian romance to be presented in novel form. Alfred was a particular favourite of women writers, beginning with Anne Fuller's *The Son of Ethelwolf* in 1789, after which no fewer than eleven women retold Alfred's story. But male writers, too, including G. A. Henty and Gordon Stables, wrote Alfredian novels that concentrated on the king as fighter rather than lover.

LOSING ALFRED

After the celebration of the Alfred millenary in 1901, the flood of creative writing on the king slowed to a trickle, but elements of the mythical Alfred can be seen in the more faithfully 'historical' work of Alfred Duggan or Basil Bonallack (whose novel *Flame in the Dark* was published in 1976), as well as more recent imagined Alfreds such as Joan Wolf's in *The Edge of Light* (1990) or Bernard Cornwell's series of novels beginning with *The Last Kingdom* (2004). The only film about Alfred may be risible as a piece of cinema, but it is remarkable how many of the traditional elements of the mythical Alfred it preserves, even if there is no room for the cakes.

We have already noticed (in Chapter 8) a similarity to John Home's *Alfred: A Tragedy,* in the Danish camp scene, but our first encounter with Alfred, as he prepares to be ordained, recalls Wordsworth's king, 'a pupil of the monkish Gown'; while the involvement of West Saxon women at Edington evokes Aethelflaed's defence of her appearance in military garb in an anonymous play of 1753, *Alfred the Great, Deliverer of his Country.* Our heroine tells us that we should not doubt that 'Dames of old / Would quit their petticoats, and put on Breeches, / Or risk their Lives; ... they were cunning Witches. / Breeches they wore, and very oft wou'd rent 'em; / And who, besides their Husbands, wou'd prevent 'em?'

The legend of Alfred seems to have passed comprehensively in the past two or three decades from novelists, poets and even film-makers to historians and archaeologists. Anyone attempting today to base a narrative on the life of Alfred has far less of a shared set of myths to draw on, and even the story of the cakes is not as well remembered today as it was forty years ago. Thackeray, whom we have already encountered more than once using the public rehashing of Alfred as a butt of humour, summed up the irony of the folk-tale hero giving way to the historians more than a hundred years ago in one of 'Miss Tickletoby's lectures on English history'.

For a thousand years, these little tales have passed from father to son all through England, and every single man out of millions and millions who has heard them has loved King Alfred in his heart, and blessed him, and was proud that he was an Englishman's king. And then he hears that Alfred fought the Danes, and drove them out of England, and that he was merciful to his enemies, and

28. Fallen idol: putting up Thornycroft's statue in Winchester was hard work. First, the 28lbs of sugar used to settle the upper granite monolith on the lower attracted a swarm of bees and halted proceedings, then the guy-ropes for the figure itself snapped, injuring the contractor

kept faith at a time when everyone else was deceitful and cruel, and that he was the first to make laws, and establish peace and liberty among us.

For a long time the serious historian of Alfred has had to contend first with the reading public's belief in the 'little tales' that followed Asser, and then with a number of a-historical notions about Alfred's achievements. Now, however, dismissal of all these has left a king practically unknown outside academe, though better understood than ever within it.

Stories – some without foundation, some not contemporary, others wrongly authorised and rightly dismissed – represent a way of thinking about the king that would be pointless as an end in itself but that has served as an inspiration to deeper thinking to 'millions and millions'. As Chesterton put it: 'That is the use of tradition; it telescopes history.'

FURTHER READING

As it has been part of the purpose of this book to show, the number and variety of books and other materials about or inspired by King Alfred are practically unlimited. There are both printed and on-line bibliographies available for those who would go into the subject at much greater depth. For example, there is J. T. Rosenthal, *Anglo-Saxon History: An Annotated Bibliography 450–1066* (1985); the annual Cambridge *Anglo-Saxon England* includes a bibliography of each year's scholarly works; and Simon Keynes's website http://www.trin.cam.ac.uk/sdk13/ also contains links to various bibliographies, including his own.

But the best place to start is with the contemporary sources in which Alfred's reign – relatively speaking – abounds. *Alfred the Great: Asser's 'Life of King Alfred' and Other Contemporary Sources* (1983), edited by Simon Keynes and Michael Lapidge, contains a full translation of Asser, those parts of the Chronicle not reproduced in Asser, as well as the Burghal Hidage, selections from Alfred's own writings, and extracts from his law code and his will. The introduction and notes are an excellent way into not just modern Anglo-Saxon scholarship but also a consideration of the historical 'cult' of King Alfred. There is an appendix on the story of the cakes, with translations from the various early versions. The other essential volume of source material, with a complete version of the Chronicle (with variations) for the relevant years, as well as some letters and extracts not found in Keynes and Lapidge, is Dorothy Whitelock's *English Historical Documents*, vol. 1, *c. 500–1942* (2nd edn, 1979).

For the background to Alfred's Wessex and his reign, F. M. Stenton's volume on *Anglo-Saxon England* in the Oxford History of England (1943; 3rd edn, 1971) is still very much worth looking at, as is Peter Hunter Blair's *Introduction to Anglo-Saxon England* (1956; 3rd edn, 2003). The three authors of *The Anglo-Saxons* (1982) – James Campbell, Eric John and Patrick Wormald – were all leaders in their field, and Wormald's chapter on Alfred and the ninth century is as thought-provoking and informative an introduction to the period as anyone could wish for.

Alfred is the Anglo-Saxon king with by far the most biographies to his name. Earlier twentieth-century ones such as those by Charles Plummer (1902) and Beatrice A. Lees (1915) – whose title *Alfred the Great, the Truthteller* demonstrates a commitment to a specific aspect of Alfred's myth – are still worth looking at. The best short introduction is now Patrick Wormald's entry in the *Oxford Dictionary of National Biography* (2004), which treats the subject with respect but not reverence. Most recently, Richard Abels's compact but impressively comprehensive *Alfred the Great: War, Kingship and Culture in Anglo-Saxon England* (1998) takes a more measured tone than Alfred P. Smyth's weighty *King Alfred the Great* (1995), much of which is devoted to 'proving' Asser to be a medieval forgery. Smyth's inclusion of almost all the evidence at his disposal does not make for easy reading, but his willingness to question notions about Alfred that even more sceptical scholars were reluctant to reconsider deserves admiration. His deep knowledge of the Viking material gives the book a more balanced feel than its contemporaries. Another life published in the same year, by the archaeologist David Sturdy, is idiosyncratic but far more readable than Smyth. Justin Pollard's new biography *Alfred the Great: The Man Who Made England* (2005) appeared just too late to be consulted for this book.

When thinking about the king's childhood and children's stories of it, I looked as well at Charles Dickens's *A Child's History of England* (1851–3), the Ladybird *King Alfred the Great*, by L. du Garde Peach (1956), R. J. Unstead's *People in History* (1957) and H. E. Marshall's *Our Island Story* (1905; reissued 2005). A sassy modern Alfred is portrayed in Terry Deary's *Smashing Saxons* (2002). Alfred's trip to Rome was considered by Janet Nelson in an essay collected in her *Politics and Ritual in Early Medieval Europe* (1986) and revisited in an essay, 'The Franks and the English in the Ninth Century Reconsidered' (1991), which leaned towards the view that the letter from Pope Leo (in Whitelock, *EHD*, vol. 1) is genuine (discussed by Abels). For artistic renditions of Alfred, see Roy Strong, *And When Did You Last See Your Father?* (1978; reprinted in 2004 as *Painting the Past*), and Simon Keynes's website listed above, which also contains a very full list of paintings, sculptures etc. on the subject of Alfred, helpfully divided into themes. For Archbishop Parker, see Edith Weir Perry, *Under Four Tudors* (1964).

The Vikings have received an upsurge of popular and academic interest. Among the best introductions are *The Oxford Illustrated History of the Vikings* (1997), edited by Peter Sawyer, whose general 'rehabilitation' of the Vikings in various works since the early 1960s has been influential. Alfred Smyth's *Scandinavian Kings in the British Isles* (1971) makes careful use of the sagas to paint a more violent picture. The sagas themselves and other sources are collected and discussed in R. I. Page's *Chronicles of the Vikings: Records, Memorials and Myths* (1995). Viking re-enactment, emphasising the 'good side' of the Viking 'legacy', is a phenomenon best observed on the web (if not donning helmet and shield): see, for example, www.vikingsonline.org.uk. For the beginnings of the Scandinavian revival in the eighteenth century see Rosemary Sweet, *Antiquaries: The Discovery of the Past in Eighteenth Century Britain* (2004).

Alfred the soldier and general is discussed by Abels in his *Lordship and Military Obligation in Anglo-Saxon England* (1988), and by John Peddie in *Alfred the Good Soldier* (1989; later re-published as *Alfred: Warrior King*). Alfred Smyth considers the evidence that Alfred may have been a subject king to the Vikings at some time between 871 and 878.

The cakes and Athelney are, of course, the focus of the greatest amount of more or less helpful comment and discussion. The appendix to Keynes and Lapidge contains references to the original sources of the story. A Historical Association pamphlet by Robert Birley entitled *The Undergrowth of History: Some Traditional Stories of English History Reconsidered* (1955) takes a benign view of the value of stories in history and their genesis, though Birley thought that the Life of St Neot was 'lost' (it was printed in 1809 and has been again, with the Annals of St Neots, in an edition published in 1985). An interesting consideration of the literary sources and implications of the tale is in Joaquín Martínez Pizarro, 'Kings in Adversity: A Note on Alfred and the Cakes', *Neophilologus*, 80/2, pp. 319–26 (1996). William of Malmesbury's *Gesta Regum Anglorum* has been translated with very complete annotation by R. A. B. Mynors, R. M. Thomson and M. Winterbottom (1998). The 1778 edition of *Alfred: A Masque,* expanded so that the greater part is by Mallet, provides the quotations from the talkative shepherd.

The influence of the cakes story and its rebuttal by scholars can be seen in W. H. Stevenson's edition of Asser (1904; reprinted 1959), Charles Plummer's *The Life and Times of Alfred the Great* (1902), R. H. C. Davis's 'Alfred the Great: Propaganda and Truth' (1971), collected in *From Alfred the Great to Stephen* (1991), and Dorothy Whitelock's 'The Importance of the Battle of Edington' (1977), a reply to Davis printed in *From Bede to Alfred* (1980). The events and speeches of the Alfred millenary at Winchester were recorded by their organiser, mayor Alfred Bowker, in *The King Alfred Millenary: A Record of the National Commemoration* (1902). An exploration of the power of combinations of myth, fiction and history for a different time and place can be seen in Simon Schama's *Dead Certainties (Unwarranted Speculations)* (1991).

R. H. C. Davis and Richard Abels's works mentioned above are helpful for the Burghal Hidage and Alfred's defensive measures. The essays in *The Defence of Wessex* (1996), edited by David Hill and Alexander R. Rumble, go into more detail, and an illustration of close correlation between wall lengths and hidage is given in *An Atlas of Anglo-Saxon England* (1981), by David Hill.

For Alfred and the law see Patrick Wormald's magisterial *The Making of English Law: King Alfred to the Twelfth Century,* vol. 1 (1999); the second volume, which promised further discussion of Alfred and his successors' law in practice and their legacy has not appeared, though references in the first imply that the author's work on it must have been advanced at his untimely death in 2004. Whitelock and Keynes and Lapidge include Alfred's law code in their selections, and the Fonthill Letter is in Whitelock.

The fruits of Alfred's scholarly activities are not easy to taste in their entirety. Keynes and Lapidge and Whitelock all include extracts from the king's translations, and *The Whole Works of King Alfred the Great* (1852; reprinted 1969) makes some now outdated assumptions about the corpus of Alfredian translation. T. A. Shippey's article 'Wealth and Wisdom in King Alfred's Preface to the Old English Pastoral Care' (*English Historical Review*, 94, 1979) started a new strand of thinking on the purposes and language of the programme. But see also Allen J. Frantzen, *King Alfred* (1986) for the importance of 'warfare and wisdom'. Frantzen's clear and informative book gives a good general summary and commentary. Articles by Janet Bately, Simon Keynes and Malcolm Godden in *Alfred the Great: Papers from the Eleventh Centenary Conferences* (2003), edited by Timothy Reuter, put forward the latest ideas about the extent, purpose and content of the Alfredian literary renaissance. V. H. Galbraith's 1964 article 'Who Wrote Asser's Life of Alfred?' can be found in *An Introduction to the Study of History*. Though Dorothy Whitelock's *The Genuine Asser* (1968) held the field for many years, Alfred Smyth's comprehensive attack in his biography, followed up by his own edition of Asser, received various rebuttals, one of which, Michael Lapidge's, in an appendix to his essay on 'Asser's Reading' in the Reuter volume already mentioned, contains the dread warning about ignorance of Latin.

Abels and Keynes and Lapidge ably disentangle Asser's confusing portrait of Alfred's sicknesses. Michael Wood's suggestions of a 'psycho-sexual' element can be found in his essay 'The Case of the Fenland Forger' in *In Search of England* (1999). For a more vigorous, less ill king, see Smyth's *King Alfred the Great*.

The cult and afterlife of the king are discussed by Keynes and Lapidge in their introduction and greatly expanded on by Simon Keynes in his 'The Cult of King Alfred the Great' in *Anglo Saxon England 28* (2000), edited by Michael Lapidge, Malcolm Godden and Simon Keynes. Keynes's essay is the source of the quotation about stripping and clearing away preconceptions etc. in my introduction, and a mine of examples of which I have made repeated use. Bowker contains many statements of the 'maximalist' view of Alfred as multiple founder. Alfred, England and Englishness and their antecedents have received scholarly and non-jingoistic attention from Patrick Wormald, in for example, 'Bede, the *Bretwaldas* and the Origins of the *gens anglorum*' in *Ideal and Reality in Frankish and Anglo-Saxon Society* (1983). That book was a Festschrift for J. M. Wallace-Hadrill, the godfather of the idea of Alfred as a king in Carolingian company and author, for example, of *Early Germanic Kingship in England and the Continent* (1971). Janet Nelson's work is also instructive in this context. For a recent view of Alfred as the father of English identity, which is none the less alive to the continental perspective, see Sarah Foot, 'The Making of *Angelcynn*: English Identity before the Norman Conquest' (*Royal Historical Society Transactions*, 6th series, 6, 1996).

For the naming of the US Continental Navy ship *Alfred* see, for example, James Mackay, *I Have Not Yet Begun To Fight: A Life of John Paul Jones* (1998). Barbara Yorke's essay in the Reuter eleventh-centenary conference volume discusses the wider impact of the Winchester millenary, as does Paul Readman's 'The Place of the Past in English Culture *c*. 1890–1914', in *Past and Present*, 186 (2005).

For references to literary Alfreds see also Eric Stanley, 'The Glorification of King Alfred in Literature', in *A Collection of Papers with Emphasis on Old English* (1987) and L. W. Miles, *King Alfred in Literature* (1902). Bernard Cornwell's novel *The Last Kingdom* (2004) is the first of a new series on Alfred and his time; the second is *The Pale Horseman* (2005). Elfrida Manning's biography of Hamo Thornycroft, *Marble and Bronze* (1982) contains his conversations with the mayor and the electrician, and G. F. Watts is discussed by Roy Strong, and by Janet McLean in 'Watts, Historical Thought and the Schemes of Painting in the 1840s', in *Representations of G. F. Watts: Art Making in Victorian Culture (British Art and Visual Culture since 1750* (2004), edited by Colin Trodd and Stephanie Brown. The film *Alfred the Great* is mercifully not available as a recording but is a favourite of very late night television schedulers.

LIST OF ILLUSTRATIONS

While every effort has been made to contact copyright-holders of illustrations, the author and publishers would be grateful for information about any illustrations where they have been unable to trace them, and would be glad to make amendments in further editions.

ACKNOWLEDGEMENTS

Charles Plummer complained in 1901 of being 'more than a little jealous that the greatest name in English history should be considered a theme on which any one may try his prentice hand'. I have been acutely aware during the writing of this book that Alfred is indeed an unwise choice for a first-time author, but help and support from all quarters have encouraged me to persevere. The greatest thanks go to my wife, Jules, to whom this book is dedicated and without whom it would have been inconceivable. Her confidence that I could write it eventually rubbed off on me. Her indulgence for our detours to Winchester, Athelney and other points West was never strained. My son Jude has seen far too many ninth-century treasures in his two years, and never complained. My interest in Anglo-Saxon history, and dim understanding of its complexities and implications, were kindled by the late Patrick Wormald, whose advice I would have valued most highly, but whose mighty example I tried, however falteringly, to keep in mind.

Mary Beard and Peter Carson have been ideal editors, while Penny Daniel and Nicola Taplin have handled irritating requests with kind expertise. At the TLS, my editor Peter Stothard has turned a benignly blind eye to Alfredian obsessions, and my colleagues, especially Robert Potts and

Adrian Tahourdin, have never failed to ask how 'King Arthur and the cakes' was coming along. Martin Smith's help with picture research was invaluable. The staffs of the British, London and Hackney Central Libraries have all come to my aid in different ways.

Richard Gameson, of the University of Kent, kindly and diligently read the typescript and saved me from my most egregious errors (any which remain are, of course, my responsibility). I have benefited from discussions with and suggestions from Mark Bostridge, Rupert Shortt and not least, my mother and father. Amanda Lockhart professionally took my photograph for a less than professional fee.

INDEX